LETTERS
ON
CEYLON
PARTICULARLY RELATIVE
TO THE
KINGDOM OF KANDY

LETTERS
ON
CEYLON
PARTICULARLY RELATIVE
TO THE
KINGDOM OF KANDY

ILLUSTRATED WITH A SURVEY OF KANDY

CAPT. L. DE BUSSCHE

GYAN

Published by

Gyan Publishing House
5, Ansari Road
Daryaganj, New Delhi-110002
Phone: 011-47034999, 9811692060
E-mail: books@gyanbooks.com

Distribution Network
gyanbooks.com
India, USA, Canada, UK, Australia, France

ISBN : 978-81-212-3701-7 (PB)
First Published, London, 1817

2nd Impression 2020

Printed at: Gyan Press, Delhi.

Letters on Ceylon Particularly Relative to the Kingdom of Kandy
Author: Capt. L. De bussche

LETTERS

ON

CEYLON;

PARTICULARLY RELATIVE

TO THE

KINGDOM OF KANDY.

BY

CAPTAIN L. DE BUSSCHE,

Late Acting Deputy Adjutant General in Ceylon.

Illustrated with a Survey of Kandy.

LONDON:

Printed for J. J. STOCKDALE, No. 41, Pall Mall

1817.

PREFACE

The three first of the following letters, and part of the fourth, were originally written to a friend for his private information. The Author (lately returned to England) having been advised to publish them, has, with that view, completed the fourth, and made some few alterations in the rest.

He is aware that the public do not take that interest in what relates to Ceylon which a colony so valuable deserves; and though he is far from presuming that these letters will be the means of increasing that interest, he trusts that many families who have friends and relations in that island will be gratified by their perusal.

The situation of the Author for several years in Ceylon, enabled him to collect, at least correct, information little known till now respecting Kandy, and the interior provinces, and to remove those apprehensions which have prevailed as to the insalubrity of the climate.

It is to the numerous friends of Lieutenant-General Sir Robert Brownrigg that these letters are particularly offered. To them all the good Sir Robert has done in the Island of Ceylon, and all the benefit and credit he has rendered to his country, however imperfectly described, cannot fail to be acceptable.

By his mild and just sway that Island promises to become as valuable to the crown of Great Britain, as his government has proved to be a blessing to its inhabitants.

Deficient as the expression of his sentiments towards this good and respectable character may be, there is no one of his numerous or oldest friends who can cherish for him more attachment, esteem, and admiration than is felt by the writer of these letters.

The indulgence of the public and of critics (if the latter should deign to peruse his work) for any inaccuracies of the composition, is earnestly requested. The Author has written in a language which is not his own, and has necessarily had to struggle with great difficulties. Whatever the fate of this publication may be, it will at any rate have yielded the writer one high source of gratification in the opportunity it has given him to pay a small tribute of gratitude and respect to the present excellent and honorable Governor of Ceylon, under whom it has been his happiness to serve.

"Gratulor quod eum quem necesse erat diligere, qualiscunque esset, talim habemus ut libenter quoque diligamus."—*Treb. apud Tull.*

CONTENTS.

LETTER I.—PAGE 1.

LETTER II.—Page 54.

LETTER III.—Page 77.

LETTER IV.—PAGE 116.

APPENDIX.—PAGE 145.

ERRATA.

Page	Line	
43	21,	read *Budhu*, for *Budha.*
50	20,	*Nalande*, for *Nalude.*
50	20,	*Amenapoora*, for *Aminapoora.*
51	19,	*street*, for *streets.*
53	4,	*head*, for *ear.*
63	1,	*twelfe*, for *fifteen.*
63	4,	*Thoen* for *Thorn.*
78	16,	*posts*, for *parts.*
79	19,	*or you see*, for *or to see.*
81	9,	*Oudanowera*, for *Oudanwera.*
97	9,	*on Ceylon*, for *to Ceylon.*
104	10,	*Probolingo*, for *Prabolingo.*
121	10,	£309,000, for 230,000.

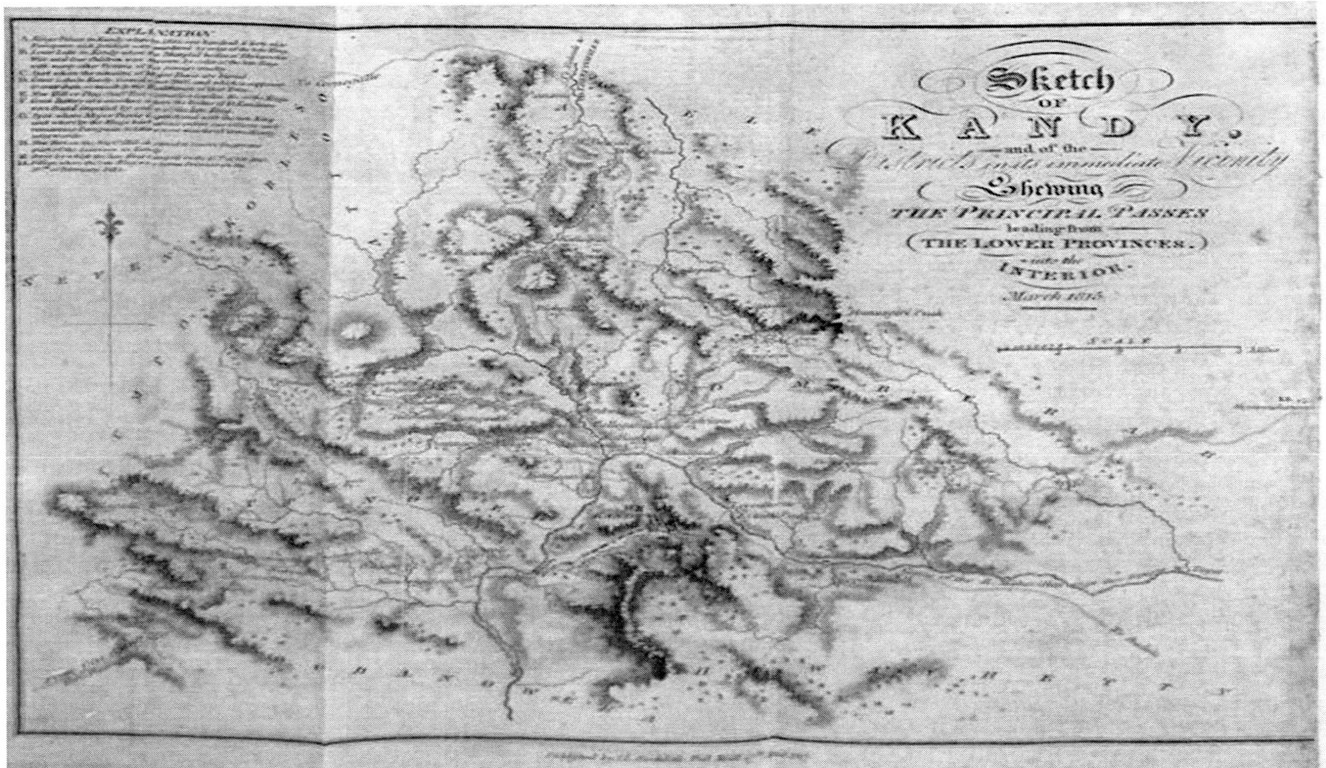
Sketch
OF
KANDY.
and of the
District in its immediate Vicinity
Shewing
THE PRINCIPAL PASSES
leading from
THE LOWER PROVINCES,
into the
INTERIOR.
March 1815.
EXPLANATION
SCALE

TRANSACTIONS

IN

KANDY.

LETTER I.

Columbo, Island of Ceylon,
19th June 1815.

DEAR SIR,

MORE than eight months have elapsed since my last letter was written; and although I am well aware that the public prints must, long before this, have informed you, generally, of our military operations in this Island, yet our success has been so complete, and its results so important, that I cannot deny myself the pleasure of giving you a more ample detail

 of

of our short, but effective campaign. The conquest of an extensive, rich, and beautiful country; its annexation to the British crown; and the downfal of one of the most savage and wanton tyrants that Providence ever permitted, for a time, to scourge the human race, have been achieved in forty days, without the loss, on our side, of a single man.

> " A victory is twice itself, when the achiever
> " Brings home full numbers."
>
> *Shakespeare.*

The cruel career of Vikrimi Rajah Singa (for such is the name of the deposed King of Kandy) is at an end, and his perfidious and inhuman conduct towards the sickly and enfeebled garrison at Kandy in 1803, in breach of a solemn treaty, at length amply avenged. The country, which he held by usurpation, and which groaned under his misrule, hails its deliverers. It is ours, both by the dominion of arms

and

and the ascendancy of opinion, and the tyrant himself is a prisoner in this fort.

My last letter told you, that a small corps of observation was formed in November last, under the command of Major Hook, second Ceylon regiment; it was shortly afterwards ordered to Hangwell, a small fort in our old territory, and thence to Avisahwelle, a village on our frontier, about thirty miles from Columbo.

Other corps, from different points, as I shall state hereafter, were ordered to be held in readiness for service.

These preparations were imperiously called for by the outrageous and barbarous conduct of the King of Kandy towards some of our unoffending subjects, who had passed the frontier for the purposes of trade, as they had been accustomed to do, under the implied sanction of his government, and at a time when no misunderstanding with our own had been avowed, and when no provocation had been given or meditated. The necessity of these preparations became more pressing, from the increasing disaffection of his own subjects, alienated by his oppression, and looking towards us as their only source of relief. Amongst the many and flagrant instances of cruelty and injustice which this monster was daily guilty of, I will only mention three of the most prominent. Pelame Talawa, the first *Adikar* (or Minister), by whose assistance the tyrant had usurped the throne, and who at all times had served him faithfully, was, in the year 1809, on some frivolous pretence, treacherously murdered. To him succeeded Eheylepola as *Adikar*, whose influence for a while was considered unbounded. He, however, in the course of last year, fell under the displeasure of his master, and was ordered to court, to answer a complaint urged against him in his absence. Well knowing what the consequence of such a summons would be, whether

ther guilty or innocent, he retired into the province of Saffragam, of which he was also *Dessave* or chief. There he assembled his friends, with a view to resistance, but being defeated, he fled into the British territory for protection. Had he fallen into the hands of his offended sovereign, his rebellion might have justified the utmost severity; but who can read, without shuddering with horror, of the revenge which was inflicted by this monster on the *Adikar's* guiltless family, who, according to the custom of the court of Kandy, had been detained at the capital as hostages for his fidelity!

The wife of Eheylepola, and his four children were butchered in the presence of the King, with every refinement of cool-blooded cruelty. The infants were decapitated in the presence of their agonized mother, who was then forced to pound their bleeding heads in a mortar. After this, her own throat was cut, and the body, with the remains of her children, cast into the lower tank of Kandy.

The third instance almost equals in atrocity the last, and is what I have just noticed as the operative cause of our preparations for war; which by this act became unavoidable, with any regard to national honor and the protection due to those under our allegiance. Ten native merchants, our subjects, regular traders in cotton cloths, &c. passed the limits of the Kandian territories, about twelve months ago (July 1814), as they had been allowed to do for the last ten years, when on a sudden they were seized, accused of being spies, and without any trial, in the presence of the King, mutilated in the most horrid manner. Their noses were first cut off, and then an arm and an ear of each. Seven of these unfortunate sufferers died under the operation, or in consequence of it: three alone survived to reach

reach our frontier, and announce the fate of their companions and themselves.

These and other such acts of ferocious despotism produced applications to our government for protection and assistance, from many quarters; not only from our own subjects, but also from numerous bodies of Kandians. Discontent and disturbances prevailed in all the Kandian provinces, which induced our Governor to order Major Hook's corps to that frontier, in the neighbourhood of which the King of Kandy's troops, and the insurgents under Eheylepola, were principally assembled.

The necessity of a war gained every day strength, and it became more urgent to make preparations for offensive operations. Our means were, comparatively speaking, few, not only in the number of disposable troops, but also for the conveyance of ammunition and provisions. To increase the former, an application had

 been

been made to the government of Madras for about two thousand five hundred men, which were readily promised, and actually put in motion to join us; and in furtherance of the latter, the civil officers of government, in particular the collectors of districts (as more nearly connected with our field operations) assembled, by incessant labour, the necessary number of camp followers and bullocks for the transport of ammunition, camp equipage and provisions, and thus enabled the different corps to take the field. I need not say, that every officer and soldier hailed with satisfaction the order which was now issued to prepare for field service.* There were indeed not wanting persons who, from past experience,

---

* This order was not issued till the 21st of November 1814, months after the outrage committed on our subjects; so that full time was given to the tyrant of Kandy to have explained this act, had it admitted of explanation, or had he been disposed to give it.

experience, and reverting to former misfortunes, were adverse to the expedition; but I must render justice to every one in Ceylon by saying, that whatever their private opinions might be, as to the impolicy or danger of the measure, it had no effect in diminishing their exertions to forward the views of our excellent general. A personal experience of nearly four years had taught them that, to carry into effect the orders of such a man as General Brownrigg, could only tend to promote public welfare.

His Excellency set a noble example to us all. He had undertaken an expedition, in which so many had failed. The disasters which had attended the campaign of 1803, which were known and felt by every one, must have pressed with peculiar weight on the mind of him, with whom the whole responsibility of the measure rested; but an imperious call of duty obliged him to enter

enter on this war. His Majesty's subjects had been mutilated or murdered by the tyrant of Kandy, during a time of profound peace, and several entire provinces of that unfortunate country had implored the protection of our arms, and made a voluntary offer of allegiance to Great Britain, to free them from the miseries by which they were surrounded. The orders which His Excellency gave to prepare the troops for field service, evinced all that paternal care and foresight which so much distinguish his measures, and were calculated to insure comfort and health to officers and men.

The General superintended, by almost daily inspection, the outfit of the several corps from Columbo; not even a most painful illness, which would have kept most other men in their beds prevented his attendance on his numerous and increasing duties. He was one of the first who took the field, and latterly

latterly his head-quarters were fixed with the second division, not surrounded by the luxuries of an Asiatic camp, but participating in the passing wants of the officers serving under him. Such conduct on his part was calculated to, and did, animate them, neither to think on the dangers of the war, nor on those of the climate; but to be always ready to make every effort to forward the plans of their General, to whom they were attached by that feeling which is not transitory, a love founded on respect.

Forewarned, then, as we were, that few of us would return from this service, we all, emulating the example of our General, cheerfully prepared for it; and if you will consider that scarce any of our officers or men had seen actual service, you will give them the more credit for their promptitude in taking the field.

Where every officer did his duty so well, I should feel a reluctance to discriminate

any,

any, if I were not assured that all will at least approve of my selecting three names as entitled to peculiar notice. In a country like Kandy, with no better road than a bridle path, and that frequently leading over difficult passes and high mountains; where all military stores and provisions must necessarily be transported by men, one of the great difficulties of carrying on war is the danger of starving; it requires, therefore, more than ordinary attention and exertion in the commissariat to obviate so serious an evil. This was well guarded against by Colonel Kerr, the officer at the head of that department in our old provinces, and subsequently by Major Hardy (military Secretary to his Excellency the Governor) in the newly acquired provinces. To their exertions in preparing, collecting, and forwarding the supplies of all kinds for the different corps and garrisons, is owing that the troops were constantly well supplied with

with abundance of wholesome food, whereby one of the principal causes of the miseries which befell our army in 1803 was obviated. By Major Willerman, the Deputy Quarter-master General here, whose indefatigable enquiries and observations enabled him to gain a correct knowledge of the enemy's country, the different divisions of the army were supplied with excellent charts, and the most distinct information respecting the strength of the passes leading into the interior, till then considered as impregnable; such as the Balany and Idalgalsinia Pass. To his exertions every possible praise is due. With great justice, General Brownrigg placed the utmost confidence in the experience of this scientific officer, in whose extended mind and powers of combination resources were found for most of our wants, and I can assure you they were numerous.

The

The plan for attacking Kandy was a-ranged on the supposition that about two thousand five hundred effective men would arrive from the coast, and the strength of the different divisions was prepared accordingly.

Two divisions from Columbo consisting of about six hundred men each; two divisions from Galle and Matura, of about five hundred men each; two divisions from Trincomalee, of about four hundred men each; and a detachment from Batticaloo of about two hundred men, were the corps to be furnished by the army in Ceylon. The troops from the coast were to march in two divisions from Putlam and Negombo, each of six hundred men, leaving the rest of their force as a reserve in garrisons on the west coast of Ceylon, from Columbo to Jaffnapatam. The different routes were to bring them at a given period to the neighbour-hood

hood of Kandy, leaving a sufficient detached force in their rear to establish posts for a secure communication with their resources, to open roads, &c.

These orders were issued, and all arrangements made nearly to this effect, when unexpectedly, in the beginning of January, an express arrived from the Madras government, informing General Brownrigg, *that the promised force could not be spared, and was countermanded.* I *must* refrain from making any observations on this unexpected proceeding, and leave it for better judges to divine how far the absence of two thousand five hundred men could at that time have interfered with any political arrangement of the Honorable Company in India. As affairs have turned out, it matters not; but at the time it was a circumstance calculated to create difficulty and despondence, and it was only by one who possessed strong re-

sources

sources within himself that it could be treated as a matter of indifference. By a singular coincidence of circumstances it so happened that on the same day this news arrived, 11th January 1815, (and it came by a sea conveyance after a very short passage) the King of Kandy's troops passed our frontiers, and committed many and serious depredations on our subjects. This obliged his Excellency the Governor to issue a declaration of war. *

The absence of the auxiliary force from Madras occasioned some change in the formation of the different divisions, as it was necessary to make a new arrangement to supply the place of two divisions of Madras troops, which were intended to have marched from Putlam and Negombo.

The disposable force was ultimately divided as follows.

First

* See Appendix, No. 1.

First division, or advance from Columbo, four hundred and thirty men, commanded by Major Hook, second Ceylon regiment.

Second division,or reserve from Columbo, seven hundred and eighty men, commanded by Lieutenant Colonel O'Connell, seventy-third regiment; his advance by Major Moffatt, first Ceylon regiment.

Third division, or advance from Galle, four hundred and two men, commanded by Major Kelly, fourth Ceylon regiment.

Fourth division, or reserve from Galle and Hambantotte, six hundred and forty-two men, commanded by Colonel Alexander Macgregor Murray, fourth Ceylon regiment; his advance by Major M'Donald, nineteenth regiment:

Fifth division, or advance from Trincomalee, four hundred and forty-five men, commanded by Major Mackay, third Ceylon regiment.

Sixth

Sixth division, or reserve from Trincomalee; five hundred men, commanded by Major General Jackson, and under him by Colonel Rainsford, nineteenth regiment.

Seventh division, from Batticaloo, two hundred and five men, commanded by Captain Anderson, nineteenth regiment.

Eighth division, from Negombo, two hundred and twenty men, commanded by Captain de Bussche, aid-de-camp to Lieutenant General Brownrigg, to which were added a free corps of Malays, raised by that officer, which augmented this force to three hundred and forty men.

Immediately following the declaration, the corps of Major Hook engaged the enemy and drove him, after a slight resistance, from the post at Ruanwelle, situated at the river Kalane-ganga; here a post was immediately established, and a situation traced out by Major Willerman for the building of a fort, as the possession of this place insured

insured to us a safe and commodious conveyance of all our provisions from Columbo, by boats on the Kalane-ganga, for a distance of forty-two miles, towards Kandy. The rapidity of the river also enabled us, in case of need, to send our sick men in nine hours to Columbo. Large magazines of all kinds were here formed, which retarded the advance of the first division for some days, and enabled the other divisions, which were more distant, to arrive near their points of debouchement.

On the 29th of January this division forded the river Maha Oya; it required only a few shots to drive the enemy from a battery near that river. On the same day a party of riflemen under the command of Lieutenant Mylius, first Ceylon regiment, composing the advanced guard of the eighth division, had an engagement with the Kandians, who were defeated, with the loss of six men killed, several wounded and made prisoners ; some arms, and a large store of paddy (rice in the husk) were captured at the King's garden, called Nahagederah Attua, near Wissenave.

On the 31st of January, two small detachments, under the command of Captain Parker and Lieutenant Reed, second Ceylon regiment, of the first division, surprised a Kandian post ; thirty of the enemy were put to the bayonet, and three prisoners and twenty stand of arms brought in ; the latter had evidently belonged to the unfortunate soldiers of the nineteenth regiment, who were massacred in and near Kandy, in 1803.

On the 2d of February the difficult pass on the Balany mountain was taken by Major Moffatt, commanding the advance of the second division. On the 3d of February Major Hook took possession of the Kandian forts of Giriahgamme and Galderah

derah (which had also been taken in 1803). On the same day the eighth division took post at Cornegall, after some slight skirmishes, in which Lieutenants Kellet, second Ceylon regiment, and Mainwaring, first Ceylon regiment, took some prisoners and arms.

The first, second, and eighth divisions, arrived on the left bank of the river Maha-villa-ganga, on the 10th and 11th of February, at a distance of from two to three miles from Kandy; on the 11th of February the King left his capital, and retired to the province of Dumbera, on the only road he conceived safe. Major Kelly (third division) had by this time, after a most difficult march, arrived at Hangeramketty, a palace to which, in former times, the kings had retired when Kandy was occupied by an enemy; Colonel Macgregor Murray (fourth division) was at Badula, and Major Mackay (fifth division) was near Panama,

 formerly

formerly Fort Macdowal. The seventh division was on its way to Bintene, and the sixth division nearly about to leave Trincomalee.

From this short sketch of our movements and operations you will observe, that the first, second, and eighth were the only divisions which saw an enemy. The few skirmishes we had can hardly be called fighting, and the cowardly conduct of our opponents can only be surpassed by their ignorance in defending a country where almost every step might be disputed, by a handful of men of common resolution, with advantage, against any number. Their batteries are a kind of breastwork, made of three rows of posts driven, at irregular distances into the ground, the space between them being filled up with rubbish, wood, stones, earth, sods, or any thing which is at hand; from behind these defences they saluted us by a volley of small

arms

arms and gingals (small swivel guns made in the country) levelled so high that the balls passed over our heads from twenty to forty feet, and struck the trees. Although the other divisions had not the amusement of chasing such an enemy, they had by far the greater difficulties to overcome. Their divisions were prepared for service in districts less abundant in means of conveyance for ammunition and provisions; the distances of their marches to Kandy were nearly double and triple to what the first, second, and eighth divisions had to perform; but the persevering spirit, and the great exertions of the commanding officers, in which they were well assisted by every officer and man under their command, surmounted all difficulties.

On the 13th of February the advance of our troops, led by Major Brownrigg, the Deputy Adjutant General, took possession of the great Kandian battery near

 Gonoroah,

Gonaroah, and then entered the capital. At the former place they were shocked to find thirteen Kandians who had been empaled alive, by order of the tyrant; their sufferings were at an end, but they must have been great from the very distorted appearance of their muscles; a more horrid sight was probably never seen. And what were the crimes of these unfortunate men, you will ask?—they had brought intelligence to the King of the march of our several columns, and the defeat and constant flight of his own men.

On the 14th of February, his Excellency Lieutenant General Brownrigg established his head quarters in the King's palace of Kandy, and the first, second, and eighth divisions were quartered in the town, leaving strong detachments at the ferries of Gonaroah, Katugastotte, Waterpologa and towards Kundusale. It was ascertained that the King had fled, with about two hundred

dred Malabar soldiers and followers towards Tildenia, in the Dumbera province. On the 15th, a detachment was formed under Lieutenant Mylius, composed of some artillery men, with a light mountain gun, the rifle company, first Ceylon regiment, and fifty men of the Malay free corps, to follow the King.

On the 16th of February, they had an engagement with a party of fifty of the King's Malabar soldiers, commanded by Mootoo Saumee, his cousin, and several other relations. They were posted on a steep rock, but Lieutenant Mainwaring attacked them with only twenty riflemen, and without firing a shot, rushed amongst them, killed and wounded several, and took seventeen prisoners;—Mootoo Saumee, and four other relations of the King, were of that number, the former refusing to surrender till he had received five wounds. This man is accused as being one of the most cruel advisers of the

the King ; his appearance is that of a ruffian. He is perfectly recovered from his slight wounds, and a prisoner here.

On the 18th of February in the evening, the King of Kandy was taken prisoner; I copy the General Order which was issued on that occasion, and which gives the best account of his capture.

GENERAL ORDERS.

Head Quarters, Kandy, 20th February, 1815.

The Commander of the Forces has the satisfaction and pleasure to anounce to the army he has the honor to command, that the King of Kandy is in our hands ; which important circumstance took place on the evening of the 18th instant, near Meyda Maha Nowera, in the Dumbera province, and was effected by the people of that province, in conjunction with some armed Kandians sent by Eheylapoola Adikar : a detachment of the first Ceylon under the command

command of Lieutenant Mylius, being in the vicinity of that place in support.

This material object being accomplished, the Lieutenant-General sincerely congratulates the troops on the successful result of their labours. It is to the zeal and ardour displayed by every officer and soldier, of every class and description, that under Providence is to be imputed the speedy and happy issue of the campaign, terminated at the end of forty days, from the time of the first division entering the Kandian territory.

The most formidable obstacles which the nature of this extraordinary mountainous country presents, have been overcome with a spirit of chearfulness and perseverance which has never been surpassed; and had the opposition, which a people attached to their Sovereign, and inhabiting a country more easy to be defended than perhaps any other in the world, been shown,

shown, Lieutenant General Brownrigg persuades himself, the troops he has the happiness to command would have acquired honour in every rencontre, and would have signalized themselves as much for their bravery, as their regular, soldier-like, good conduct has been exemplary from the day of their entering the Kandian territory. But the tyrant King, by his oppression, destroyed the attachment and affections of his subjects, who in consequence deserted him, and have generally welcomed the British troops as their deliverers. The few Malabar and other adherents of the King, whenever they have made a shew of resistance, have been put to flight, and the greater part are now prisoners of war. Thus the conquest of the kingdom of Kandy has been obtained, and the British army, who have had the good fortune to contribute to it, will be entitled to the thanks of their Sovereign and the British nation, for the

acquisition

acquisition of a possession, which, in richness and value of its productions, the importance of its geographical position as relating to British India, and natural beauty, will vie with any of the colonies belonging to the Crown of Great Britain.

The Commander of the Forces cannot conclude his Orders on this subject, without gratifying his best feelings, by expressing his entire approbation of all that has been done; and requests that Major-General Jackson, the officers in command of divisions, the heads of departments, and his personal staff, will accept his warmest acknowledgements for the able and effectual assistance they have in their several capacities afforded him, in preparing the troops for service, and conducting them under circumstances which have been attended by difficulties of no small degree. The Lieutenant General is bound to them and all the officers and soldiers of his little

army

army in gratitude, which is deeply impressed in his mind, and their prosperity will be to him an object of sincere interest during the remainder of his life.

All prisoners who may not be under sentence of a general or a regimental general court martial, to be released on the receipt of this order at the several stations, on the occasion of this success of His Majesty's Arms.

By the Lieutenant General's command,

(*Signed*) ROB. F. BROWNRIGG,
Dep. Adj. Gen.

The third and fifth divisions of the army now entered Kandy, and Major Mackay, third Ceylon regiment, was appointed commandant of that town, and of the troops ordered to remain in the new conquered provinces; these troops amount to about sixteen hundred men, including pioneers, and were distributed as follows:—

Kandy

Kandy	752 men.
Badula	348
Amenapoora...........	176
Atjale	56
Madawalatane	40
Cornegalle.............	36
Nalande	31
Hettimoelle, and Attapittia......	38
Idamalpane	27
Ruanwelle.............	63
Batugederah..........	56
Total.........	1623 men.

On the 26th of February, orders were issued to the troops not included in the above number, to return to their former garrisons.

On the second of March all the troops in and near Kandy assembled, in review order, in the great square before the palace, to celebrate the accession of the Kandian provinces

provinces to His Majesty's crown; an accession, not the result of conquest alone, but acquired in concurrence with the unanimous wish of the whole country, expressed and ratified on that day by a solemn convention, concluded between His Excellency Lieutenant General Brownrigg, Governor of Ceylon, and all the head men and priests of the Kandian provinces.

When we took possession of Kandy, not a human being was to be seen in that large city. Not a week had elapsed when many houses were again occupied by their owners, and before the second of March all the numerous streets of Kandy were filled with people, who came from distant provinces, to witness the ceremonies of that day. Early in the morning, the spacious courts of the palace began to fill with headmen, called Mohottales, Corales, Vidahns; generally speaking, men advanced in years, of good and intelligent appearance, with long black

or

or grey beards. Many of them had never seen an European face; none, or very few, any of our military; their astonishment was great when at the usual hour the daily guards were relieved. It was a fine clear day, and, by the brightness of the arms, the musick, the correct and uniform movements of the troops, their curiosity was alternately gratified. At four o'clock our friend Eheylepoola, with the first and second Adikar, and all the Dessawes, arrived with numerous retinues at the palace. The two Adikars were preceded, like the Roman consuls, by lictors, who instead of fasces were armed with immense whips made of hemp, which they constantly cracked with great noise, and which served as a warning for all the people to clear the way for them; this noise continued till they had entered the great audience hall, where a long conference took place, in which the convention was finally settled and signed by all parties, under the firing of a royal salute from the field guns drawn up in the great square.

The contrast between the reception which the transfer of the crown of Kandy to the King of Great Britain, accomplished by our arms, met with from the Kandians, with that which was given to the change of sovereignty attempted by the same means in 1803, is too striking not to be noticed. In the former case, although the King, whose pretensions we supported, was of their own religion and country, allied to their legitimate monarchs, and substituted for the same usurper we have successfully deposed, they rejected his claim. It was in vain that we placed him upon the throne of his ancestors, and surrounded it with our troops, not one chief, not a single Kandian entered the town, or gave any intimation of assent or obedience. He reigned a sovereign without subjects, in a deserted capital, till the force which had upheld him,

him, enfeebled by sickness and betrayed by perfidy, became alike incompetent to his protection or their own defence. I hope that I shall not be understood by this observation to throw any reflection upon the measures of our government at that unfortunate period. The rejection of Mootoo Saumee, and the sinister events which followed, were such as no political foresight could have anticipated; I have merely brought forward the comparison to shew how completely the late King had alienated the attachment of his subjects. At that period, he was a young man, the creature of the first Adikar, who ruled in his name. His character had not developed itself by those acts of sanguinary tyranny, which, at length, converted an entire and once loyal nation into a mass of foes.

I cannot omit mentioning here, the manner in which the High Priest of Budha, of the great temple called Maha Wehari,

hari, was ushered in, and accompanied to the audience of the Governor. About nine o'clock in the evening the Adikars and Dessaves requested leave to go to the great temple to meet the High Priest, and conduct him to the appointed meeting. Near ten o'clock * the noise of numerous tom-toms (drums of the natives in India), some fifes, trumpets, and large whips announced the approach of this interesting personage, whose influence over the opinions of the Kandians was well known to us. The spacious courts on both sides of the great audience hall were perfectly lighted up by near a thousand torches, the bearers of which preceded and followed him. The High Priest and his suite arrived under the great

* Night is considered by the Kandians as the time most proper for public ceremonies, as well of the church as of the state, and the nearer the hour approaches midnight, the more it is considered honorable to the object of the ceremony.

great portico, on the north side of the hall, which rests on twenty superb pillars, where they were received by John D'Oyly and James Sutherland, Esqrs. both of the civil service. The former gentleman was the government interpreter of the Singalese (Kandian) language, but is at present our resident in Kandy; the latter was private secretary to his Excellency the Governor, and is now secretary for the Kandian provinces. By these gentlemen the High Priest was conducted to the upper end of the hall, where General Brownrigg stood, surrounded by his general and personal staff, and a great number of officers belonging to the divisions of the army then at Kandy.

The High Priest is a man about seventy years of age, nearly five feet six inches in height; but so infirm that he is scarcely able to walk, for which reason he was supported by two young priests: about ninety priests followed in his train. On entering the hall they divided to the two sides so as to leave a large open space between them; the Dessawes stood also on each side, but nearest to the wall. The whole hall, as well the ceiling and floor, as the beautifully carved pillars, were covered with white cotton cloth. In all these arrangements the strictest Kandian court etiquette was observed. The priests were all clad in large flowing robes of rich yellow silk; that of the High Priest was of velvet of the same colour; each held a kind of fan before him, which according to their different ranks of priesthood, was more or less covered with gold, silver, or coloured silk embroidery; their heads were close shaved and uncovered. Every person having taken his station, his Excellency the Governor, in conformity to the customs and etiquette of that country, inquired, (through Mr. D'Oyly, who trans lated it to the first Adikar Molegoddi, who delivered it with a forward inclination of his

his body to the High Priest,) how his health was, hoping that the journey had not fatigued him? The High Priest expressed through the same medium his acknowledgements for the kind inquiry, which he returned with wishes for the General's welfare. He was then made acquainted with the object of the meeting, and particularly with that part of the convention which relates to the Budha religion. All the priests listened with profound attention, and after the High Priest had, for a short time, spoken in a low voice with some of the oldest about him, he returned nearly the following answer; he thanked the Governor, in the name of them all, for the protection now promised, and for that which they had already experienced; he said, that they rejoiced in the change which had lately taken place, and that he might assure the King of England of their faithful attachment: that it was greatly owing to his Excellency's mild and just government, to his benevolence to the helpless and poor, who could at all times find access to him, (which had been long known to the Kandians) that this change was effected, and therefore his arrival amongst them, had been hailed as a blessing. He added, that they knew he was a man of much religion, who feared God, and this was a sure sign that he would protect them in particular, although they were of a different religion. "We have heard," continued the venerable priest, "of your virtues, of your piety, and of your charity; and the great revolutions which have been effected among us, have had their source, not less in the admiration of your character and government, than in the evils we have suffered."

It would exceed the bounds of a letter, if I were to repeat to you the whole conversation of this interview, interesting as it it was to all of us, to see our late enemy's subjects, so fully appreciate the value of our noble and excellent commander; a better, more honorable and more virtuous man cannot exist, nor a more conscientious and faithful servant to his King and Country; and here we have a strong proof of the esteem in which these virtues were held even amongst a people whom we considered little removed from savage life, and we were highly gratified in hearing them reccognised by the chief of their priesthood in direct terms, and in such a full assembly of the principal natives.

Towards midnight the High Priest requested leave to withdraw, and I believe that we all wished him with much pleasure a good night, as the ceremonies of this day had, till that late hour, deprived us of our dinner. I must add that he begged some of our musick might precede him to his residence. The band of the third Ceylon

regiment

regiment (all Caffres) was ordered on this duty, and detained by him for some hours.

From this time until the departure of the General for Columbo, which happened on the 17th of March, we were employed to make the quarters for the troops as comfortable as possible. The hospital was established in the Queen's, or water palace, and placed under the direction of Mr. Moffatt, Surgeon to the third Ceylon regiment; to whose unremitting care, attention and ability, every possible praise is due, and much of the good health the troops have hitherto enjoyed. This gentleman is one of those few who survived the unfortunate campaign of 1803; he was then an assistant surgeon in the fifty-first regiment.

Fortifications and lines of defence were traced out, not only at Kandy, but also at Atjale, Madavalatane, Nalude, and Aminapoora, which are commanding stations at the principal passes leading to Kandy,

and

and situated in the most healthy and elevated places; the last named port is about thirteen miles from Kandy towards Columbo, at the top of the Balani pass; the situation is delightful and commands an extended view over the rich and beautiful surrounding country.

On the 20th of March, General Brownrigg arrived at Columbo. For many miles the road was covered with people anxious to see their beloved Governor again after the so much dreaded Kandian campaign. It was scarcely possible for the carriages and horses to proceed from the suburbs (where his Excellency was met by all the civil servants to government) and which extends for more than two miles from the gates of the fort; numerous triumphal arches were erected by the several casts of natives, the streets of the Moormen, or Goldsmiths, was particularly beautiful by its decorations; from the outer gate of the fortification to the government house,

house, the troops in garrison formed a street, and offered with true and heartfelt pleasure, those honors to their General which the service prescribes.

I cannot end this letter, without mentioning, that our troops, in the interior, enjoy perfect health, and we have the best prospect that they will continue to do so; very few men are in the hospital, and those are slight cases; no Jungle fever; sore legs and rheumatism are the most prevalent complaints. Only a few casualties have happened.

We have lost an officer, Major Willerman, whose death is lamented by the whole army, and by his friends more than I can describe; every person who knew him has participated in the feelings which have been so well and feelingly expressed by General Brownrigg, in a general order,* of which

* See Appendix, G. O. 13th June, 1815.

which you have here a copy. The day after the anniversary of His Majesty's birth-day, my departed friend complained of a slight pain in his ear; this uneasiness augmented the following days, and enfeebled him much; on the eleventh and twelfth of June, he had some fever, but no danger was apprehended. On the thirteenth, early in the morning, his servants called some of his most intimate friends, when they found him just closing his eyes for ever; his last moments were without pain, as his life and noble heart were without blemish.

I feel unable to add more to this letter.

Believe me, &c. &c.

LETTER II.

Columbo, Island of Ceylon, 7th July, 1816.

In resuming the subject of my last letter, in which I communicated to you the brilliant result of our short but decisive cam paign, I have sincere satisfaction in saying that the pleasing predictions which I then ventured to indulge have been more than fulfilled, by the continued good health of our troops, and the increasing attachment of the Kandians to the British government.

The recollection of the fatal campaign of 1803, will naturally have induced considerable anxiety amongst our friends in England, for the health and safety of those who are stationed in the Kandian provinces; but all apprehensions will be at an end, when they learn that, in no part of British India is the climate so wholesome as in the

the interior of Ceylon, and that our new subjects are too sensible of the advantages they enjoy, under the mild and paternal government of Sir Robert Brownrigg, to wish to revert to that state of abject slavery and dependence, from which the wisdom of his counsels, and the ability and promptitude of his military operations, have so effectually rescued them.

If you reflect in what a short period this great object was attained, without the loss of a single British soldier, that in this period, is comprised the conquest of a country nearly as large as Ireland, the overthrow of the most cruel tyrant who ever disgraced a throne, and the cheerful concurrence of the nation in the transfer of the sovereignty of an ancient and independent kingdom, to Great Britain, you will agree with me, that too much praise cannot be accorded to the distinguished officer, under whose auspices

pices such great and signal advantages have been obtained.

The precise value of our new acquisition, in a financial point of view, is even yet but imperfectly known, and you will not expect from me any minute detail of its probable resources; but, I believe, it will be found to yield, in the article of its cinnamon alone, more than sufficient to meet the expences of the civil and military establishments; the whole of the consignment of this valuable commodity, for the last and next season, having been procured from the Kandian country—its estimated value is about £100,000.

If the importance of the new territory, however, is to be estimated by the frequency of the attempts which have been made by European powers to acquire it, it will be found to be great indeed; and it is no small part of the credit attaching to our excellent commander, and to his gallant little

army,

army, that they have achieved a conquest, which has baffled the utmost exertions of the Portuguese and the Dutch for upwards of three centuries.

A short historical sketch of the incursions which have been made at several periods by European troops into the Kandian country, may not be uninteresting to you.

In the year 1517, the Portuguese, under the command of Loupo Souza de Alberganies, established themselves on the coast of the island, but their most strenuous efforts were insufficient to secure them a permanent footing in the interior. The armies they brought into the field were well disciplined, and would be considered numerous, even in the present age; and, if we reflect that the Portuguese had at that period established a high character for military prowess, their repeated failure will occasion considerable surprise. Whatever might be the success, however, which attended the commencement of the various wars into which they entered, the termination of them was uniformly disastrous, and the instances are not few in which the Kandians, after repelling the incursions of their European enemies, became in their turns the assailants, and carried terror to the gates of the principal fortresses on the coast. In the year 1590, a Portuguese army, under the command of Don Pedro de Souza, consisting of 3,788 men, of whom 1,474 were Europeans, an immense body of native allies, and a train of 1,000 elephants, sustained so signal a defeat, that few if any of the troops escaped the vengeance of their enemies.

In 1612 the Portuguese were again defeated, with a loss of 623 men killed; and on the 6th August 1614, their army, consisting of 25,000 men, was repulsed by 30,000 Kandians. In a subsequent action, towards

towards the close of the same year, they sustained another loss of 900 men. From this period till 1630, there appears to have been a cessation of active warfare; but in that year a large army, under Constantın dé Saa, was surrounded and cut to pieces in the Ouwa district: and of an army of 9,000 men which entered the Kandian country under the command of Diego de Mello, seventy only returned to Columbo; the rest having been destroyed in a pitched battle with the Kandians, who were on this occasion commanded by the Emperor Rajah Singa in person.

About 1653, the Dutch, who had some years before entered into an alliance with the King of Kandy, succeeded in finally wresting from the Portuguese their maritime possessions in Ceylon; but scarcely had they obtained possession of their new conquest, than they sought to extend it by turning their arms against their native allies. They were foiled however in every attempt, and even before the total expulsion of the Portuguese, the Dutch army, under Adrian van der Stel, had been twice defeated; first in 1644, when 688 of the Dutch troops were taken prisoners, and again in 1646, when only four men were fortunate enough to escape.

In 1670 there appears to have been a renewal of hostilities between the Kandians and the Dutch; but this war, which lasted ten years, was still more unfortunate than those which preceded it. The Dutch military force amounted to 8,000 soldiers, the strength of the enemy was computed at 153,000 fighting men. In the year 1678 Rajah Singa besieged Columbo with an army of 30,000 men; but though the total want of science and means to effect the reduction of a regular fortified place must have been apparent to the enemy himself, yet the mere circumstance of his

having

having been enabled to approach the walls of the garrison, is a sufficient proof of the ascendancy which the Kandians had gained, and of the dispiriting situation of the Dutch.

The campaign of 1765 was conspicuous only for the disasters which overwhelmed the European garrison of Kandy, few of the troops surviving the siege, during which they were for many months subjected to every species of hardship.

In 1796 the Dutch possessions in Ceylon were surrendered to the British arms ; and after a long digression we are arrived at a period in the history of Kandian affairs which can never be contemplated by our countrymen without the most painful emotions. I need not say that I allude to the fatal campaign of 1803.

I visited, with a feeling of horror, the building in the palace of Kandy, which the British had appropriated to the purposes of an hospital; for it was there that 149 European soldiers and a number of native troops were murdered, in cold blood, in their beds. The building has been rased to the ground, by order of our present Governor, and it is intended that a pillar shall be erected on the spot where it stood.

From the massacre in the hospital one European had the singular good fortune to escape. He was left for dead, but contrived to crawl to a neighbouring thicket, where he was found the following morning by the Kandians. The extraordinary circumstance of his having escaped the double peril of sickness and the sword impressed his superstitious enemies with a feeling of respect for his sufferings. They believed him favoured by a superior being, and from the moment of his being found, to the day of his deliverance, when our troops entered Kandy, including a period of fifteen years, his existence does not appear to have been embittered by any particular hardship. This man, whose name is Thorn, is living with his wife, a Kandian Moor woman, by whom he has a child, at Point de Galle, where he fills a subordinate office in the ordnance store department. It would appear that his commanding officer, Major Davies, died a natural death early in 1812, after a mournful captivity of nine years; his remains are deposited at a short distance from the town of Kandy, and a monument is to be erected there to his memory.

Independently of the loss sustained by the butchery of our unfortunate troops on this melancholy occasion, and that near the river Maha-ville-ganga, after a capitulation had been concluded, we had to regret the previous death of many brave men, who had fallen victims to the diseases then prevalent in the interior; and hence has arisen a very general impression of the utter hopelessness of any attempt to retain permanent possession of a country, the climate of which is conceived to be so prejudical to the constitution of an European.

That such a belief should have prevailed you will not be surprised at, if you refer to the accompanying return of casualties in 1803.

RETURN OF THE TROOPS SERVING ON CEYLON IN 1803.

Regiments and Corps.	Average Strength of Regiments.			Average Strength of the Troops that entered Kandy.			Deaths from the 1st of January to 30th of June 1803.
	Ser-geants.	Drum-mers.	Rank and File.	Ser-geants.	Drum-mers.	Rank and File.	
Bengal and Madras Artillery	7	4	106	4	4	60	46
Do. .. do. Gun Lascars.	14	—	386	7	—	254	18 Returns for May and June wanting.
H. M. 19th Regiment..........	49	22	751	31	12	537	175
Do. 51st do..............	51	22	547	36	12	442	214
Do. 65th do..............	10	9	152	6	3	90	93
Malay Regiment..............	51	21	885	30	18	620	80
Sepoy Regiment..............	95	38	1,712	55	22	1,049	458
Pioneer Lascars	9	—	251	5	—	171	7 { Returns for February, March, and April, wanting.
TOTAL..........	286	116	4,790	174	71	3,213	1,091

N. B.—Of the Bengal Artillery were murdered after Major Davies' Capitulation	Officers.	Serg.	R. & F.
	1	1	6
— H. M. 19th Regiment	7	9	65
— the Malay Regiment	6	24	542
— Gun Lascars [no Return].			
TOTAL...........	* 14	34	613

* This total is not included in the foregoing Return of Deaths, and most of the native soldiers, returned murdered, joined afterwards their regiment.

But if this statement, which, as you will observe, is collected from authentic sources, is calculated to excite alarm, the return of casualties for the past eighteen months is surely sufficient to dispel it, and so striking is the disproportion of deaths, that we are naturally led to inquire whether the extreme sickness with which our troops were visited in 1803, may not be attributed to causes very foreign from the mere operation of climate?

COMPARATIVE RETURN OF THE TROOPS SERVING ON CEYLON.

Regiments and Corps.	1813.		1814.		1815.		1816, 30th June.		Average Number of the Troops that have served in the Kandian Provinces, from the 1st January 1815 to the 30th June 1816.				
	Average Strength.	Deaths.	Average Strength.	Deaths.	Average Strength.	Deaths.	Average Strength.	Deaths.	Officers.	Sergeants.	Drummers.	Rank and File.	Deaths, but included in the Total for 1815 and 1816.
Europeans.													
Royal Art. 19th, 66th, and 73d Regts.	1,877	113	2,186	150	2,322	198	2,189	49		22	6	303	23
Natives.													
Gun Lascars, *Bengalis*	289	12	263	4	266	5	262	7		3	—	83	4
1st Ceylon Regt. *Malays*	700	80	1,000	16	1,096	22	1,075	7	51	12	5	238	2
2d Ceylon Regt. *Coast Sepoys*	1,023	58	1,067	35	1,043	79	993	44		2	1	52	4
3d and 4th Ceylon Regt. *Caffres*	1,186	89	1,063	76	924	60	874	34		47	18	665	38
Pioneer Lascars, *Coastmen*	1,048	43	1,076	92	1,289	92	830	21		16	1	340	23
TOTAL	5,123	395	6,655	373	6,940	456	6,223	162	51	102	31	1,681	*94

* This number is exclusive of European and native soldiers who, being taken sick at Minery (a military post near our old frontier, but now abandoned) were removed to Trincomalee and died there, and are comprehended in the total of deaths in the other parts of the island.

It must also be observed, that in the latter part of the year 1814 his Majesty's 73d regiment arrived in this island one thousand and ninety men strong, and in the beginning of 1815 about three hundred and forty recruits joined from England. These fourteen hundred men, unaccustomed to the climate, augmented the number of deaths amongst the Europeans. His Majesty's 66th regiment about the same time left this island, nearly nine hundred men strong.

The first circumstance which presents itself is the striking difference in the general comfort of the troops. Even after possession was obtained of the capital in 1803, the commissariat was so indifferently supplied, that the soldiers and camp followers were on reduced allowances. The troops were necessarily harassed by being employed in foraging parties; the paddy which was collected they were obliged to beat out before they could use, and so precarious was their remission from fatigue, and so repeated

repeated the demands on their exertions, that the time during which the soldiers were in garrison, was in fact the most arduous and distressing period of the campaign.

In 1815, the provident arrangements of General Brownrigg insured to the troops under his command every possible comfort; the country was no sooner conquered than barracks were ordered to be constructed, warm clothing distributed to the soldiers, and the most prompt measures taken that the garrisons should not be dependant on the new provinces for provisions, until experience should prove that the fidelity of our Kandian subjects might be fully relied on.

It is to these salutary precautions, dictated by that paternal care of the soldier which distinguishes General Brownrigg more than any other officer I am acquainted with, that we are to look for much of that delightful change of feeling with which

we

we now contemplate the situation of our friends in the interior of this island; and next to the reward which his own feelings will afford him, he will doubtless rank the gratitude of the many families whose relations have been spared to them by his unremitting exertions for their health and comfort.

I am ready to admit, however, that the season of 1803 may have been a particularly unhealthy one; and that some favourable circumstances may have operated in conjunction with General Brownrigg's exertions, to promote the health of the troops in 1815. With respect to the capital, a cause has been assigned for the improved salubrity of its air, which it would be unpardonable not to mention.

In the year 1803, the town of Kandy was bounded on the south by a large swamp, the noxious exhalations from which were supposed by medical men to have occasion-

ed

ed much of the disease with which our troops were at this season afflicted. To embellish his capital, by converting this swamp into two extensive sheets of water, was the favorite object of the last years of the tyrant's reign; and to gratify the fancy of the monarch, his subjects were wantonly dragged from the farthest extremity of the kingdom, and compelled to devote their gratuitous labour to the accomplishment of this great undertaking.

It is in a great measure to the abuse of power which marked the King's conduct in this instance, that the general disaffection of his subjects is to be traced; and it is a singular coincidence, that the execution of a work which has so much contributed to the health of the British troops, should have been one of the principal causes of the King's downfal.

After the fair trial we have now had of the Kandian climate, I trust we shall hear no more of those dismal forebodings with which we were assailed eighteen months ago, and that instead of anticipating disaster, we may be allowed to indulge more pleasing reflections on the value of our recent acquisition. If we regard the possession of the interior of Ceylon in a political point of view only, its importance is incalculable. Instead of having an implacable enemy in the heart of the island, ready to seize any opportunity which might offer itself for aiding the efforts of an European power, to wrest from us our maritime possessions, we have a country to retire to, so fitted by nature for defensive warfare, that a handful of troops skilfully stationed, would easily baffle the efforts of a large army; and to this we may add the co-operation of a fine race of people, who only require the incentives of a just and mild rule to become loyal and attached subjects.

It

It can scarcely be supposed that the cruelties of the late King, many and atrocious as they were, have no precedents to palliate them in the conduct of his predecessors. If you refer to Knox's Account of Ceylon, you will find that regal barbarity is an evil under which the Kandians have long groaned, and this being the case, you will probably ask, why the interference of an European power has not been solicited at an earlier period of their history?

The question would not be difficult of solution. The ill directed zeal of the Portuguese, which led them to regard a conversion to the Christian faith as a necessary test of allegiance from those over whom they exercised dominion, was of itself an insurmountable barrier to their success; and the bad faith and rapacities of the Dutch in Ceylon, and in other parts of India, had inspired the natives of the interior with a dread of their influence, which no consideration was sufficiently powerful to subdue.

The first years of Mr. North's mild administration must, no doubt, have produced a feeling of confidence and respect; but the chief Adikar was too intent on schemes of personal aggrandisement to foster any incipient feeling of cordiality towards the English; and, unfortunately, the massacre of Kandy had, at a late period, so exasperated the minds of our troops, that the partial incursions, undertaken during the two succeeding years, were of a character which must have tended to confirm the worst prejudices of the Kandians.

Under the succeeding governor the relative situation of the British and Kandians was rather an intermission of hostilities, than a restoration of peace; while political jealousy remained in full force, and little intercourse subsisted, except through the

the means of a few native traders, the Kandian people were precluded from obtaining any knowledge of the just and humane principles of British rule.

But no sooner had the full effects of Sir Robert Brownrigg's mild and equitable government been felt and acknowledged in the British provinces, than the Kandians were impatient that the blessing of his rule should be extended over their own cheerless and oppressed country. His liberality to the suffering poor in the dreadful scarcity of 1812, excited a feeling of veneration in the hearts of our natives, which it would be difficult to describe; and if ever there was an instance in which the influence of character operated in effecting a great political measure, it was in the accession of the interior provinces of the island to the crown of Great Britain.

I shall conclude what I have said on the subject of Kandian affairs, by expressing my firm conviction that the territory we have so happily gained, will be found not inferior in point of climate and natural productions to the most favoured of our other colonies, and that our new subjects will continue faithful to the allegiance they have professed, as long as the measures of the governing power are regulated by those principles of justice, moderation, and good faith, the exercise of which first attracted their respect, and conciliated their affections.

LETTER III.

Columbo, 24th July, 1816.

DEAR SIR,

My letter of the 7th inst. could scarcely have left our shores, when I received yours. I shall lose no time in answering the several questions you put to me respecting this island; although I fear that my information, on many of the topics they embrace, must necessarily be imperfect from the little connection they have with my professional pursuits.

My former letters will have given you every information respecting our military operations in Kandy, and their happy results. The garrisons, in the interior, continue to enjoy perfect health. One of the last hospital returns, which I have now before me, gives only seventy-eight men sick, out of seventeen hundred; there have been fewer, but seldom more on the sick list. Of this number twenty-seven men have sore legs, arising from the numerous leeches that attack the legs of our troops, particularly our bare-footed native soldiers employed in road making; nineteen cases of rheumatism, five of fever, three of berryberry (a species of dropsy), two of consumption, seven of bowel complaints; and the remainder suffer from diseases which a large body of troops is more or less subject to. This proportion of sick is infinitely less than at Columbo, which is considered the most salubrious garrison in all India.

The different parts in the interior are now well provided with comfortable barracks, and most of the officers and soldiers prefer to be stationed in the Kandian territory to their quarters in our old garrisons. These stations offer many and great advantages. The climate is delightful, and is often cold

cold enough of an evening to make a fire desirable. Fireplaces are beginning to be built in every room. All European vegetables thrive in the highest perfection, and in such abundance throughout the whole year, that green peas, potatoes, cabbages, turnips, carrots, &c. &c. are sent daily to Columbo, where such vegetables were seldom seen before, and never in the market. The country is beautiful beyond description—lofty mountains, covered with the finest timber, or the lesser trees and shrubs, which produce cinnamon, coffee, pepper, &c. &c. with a variety of other plants, the use and names of many of which are not even known to the botanist, are now and then separated by immense and bold masses of rock, or fine streams, on whose banks you are certain to find rich rice fields, or to see the sides of the hills cleared of woods, and brought into cultivation. These acclivities are divided into terraces, for rice fields, which assist the irrigation of the soil, so necessary for that useful grain. Some of the lesser hills and large plains are covered with the finest verdure I recollect ever having seen; this is particularly the case in the Dumbera province. A fine short grass covers the ground, and gives nourishment to numerous herds of horned cattle, the only domestic quadruped (dogs excepted) which I have met with in the interior. Sheep or goats will not thrive there; at least the few trials we have made with Jaffna sheep (the only sort in the Island) have not succeeded. I imagine that the climate is too cold, and at times too wet for them, and possibly the pastures too rich. It would be worth while to send some small Down sheep from England; if they lived they would turn to great advantage, as the meat of the Ceylon sheep is very bad.

Numerous villages are dispersed over the country, and wherever at a distance the

lofty

lofty heads of cocoa or areka trees are dispersed, you may rest assured that some dwellings are under them. The following provinces are the best inhabited, and the most fertile in rice fields :—the Seven Corles, the Dumbera Corle,* the three and four Corles, the Saffragam Corle, and the three districts near Kandy, called Yattynowera, Oudanwera, and Arispattoo.

The houses of the Kandians are far from being commodious; a very low and narrow door leads to their small rooms, and is generally the only aperture in them, except in some a small hole in the wall in lieu of a window, not large enough to admit a human head. The houses, in general, are covered with thatch; those of the headmen with tiles; the walls are of sticks and mud; stone buildings are seldom seen, and belong only to the great, but they are in the

* Corle signifies province, county, district.

the interior equally uncomfortable and dirty with those of the lowest order.

The town of Kandy is delightfully situated, and, since the draining of the swamps, has become a healthy place. The streets are broad, in straight lines, and crossing each other at right angles. The houses are low, but some of them are very extensive and built close to each other. The streets are not paved, which renders them, for a few hours after every shower, very dirty.

The King's palace is an immense pile of stone buildings, with numerous large courts. The grand temple called Maha Vihara, and a lesser one belong to it. The rooms are small, but very numerous, and amount to more than two hundred. The audience hall is a large building. The portico and inside are decorated with very fine pillars of curiously carved wood. Part of this palace is now used as a barrack; it serves also for the residence of the chief civil and military officers,

officers, and for their several offices. When we took possession of the palace all the treasures we found in it were a great number of empty boxes, some hundred earthen pots which had been in use, half a dozen broken down couches, with some paddy stampers and whips: every valuable was removed, and little has been discovered since, at least by the army. Our prize money, of which you say so much, will turn out to be a mere trifle, compared to what every person expected, from the great riches the Kings of Kandy had amassed by oppression, during several preceding centuries.

The lakes (for there are two, only divided by a strong and broad embankment built of stone) are large sheets of water. The upper lake, on which the palace for the Queen is built, contains from twenty to twenty-five acres of surface. Three sides are enclosed by stone walls, the fourth side is formed by the mountain called Kotagadolle, on which the

the flag staff fort is erected; it commands Kandy, and from it you enjoy a magnificent view. The lower lake, which is several feet below the surface of the other, covers about six or eight acres. Here the body of Ehelepoola's wife was thrown, by order of the late King, after she had been forced to destroy her four children; besides her, many other victims of the tyrant's cruelty here found a watery grave, and a deliverance from their miseries.

It is on the south side of the upper lake, in an isolated valley, where the remains of Major Davies were deposited. He died in the beginning of the year 1812, and from the description the natives give, it is imagined that a dropsy ended his days. He certainly died a natural death, in a house in the town of Kandy, which has been shewn to me, in the street called Koomaroupa, where all the King's relations resided, and where the best houses are. The last three

or

or four years of his life he enjoyed more freedom than during the first part of his captivity. He was well supplied with such necessaries of life as Kandy afforded, and I should almost think that he had become reconciled to his fate, as, after the most minute enquiry, I cannot find that he ever made any serious attempt to gain his liberty, the effecting of which, difficult as it might be, was certainly not impracticable.

I now send you a sketch of the country surrounding Kandy; I have noticed such spots as are remarkable; I wish for humanity's sake, they were less numerous; most of them are so many mementos of the cruel character of the last King.

Our newly acquired territories have hitherto been nearly unproductive of any direct revenue, although the possession of them has been the means of considerably increasing the general revenues of the island. The Custom House receipts alone, have

have exceeded, by about 200,000 rix-dollars, those of any former period of the same duration, and this is an augmentation of our resources, which may occasionally be calculated upon as progressive. The Kandians are as yet little acquainted with the good things of this world, which their intercourse with us will gradually give them a taste for. Those among them who have visited Columbo seem to relish our luxuries and admire our comforts, and some of the richer visitants have carried back with them such as they could afford to purchase. Ehelapoola made his appearance at Kandy in a single horse-chaise, which he drives about the town, to the great astonishment of the natives. His example is likely to find many imitators, though his immense riches will place him beyond the reach of competition in expenditure. I have seen this chief arrive at Columbo with nine hundred servants in his train; a retinue he may well afford, if if the report of his being in possession of the King's treasure is well founded.

It will require some time and experience before we shall be able to appreciate the resources of our new territories, so as to derive any considerable revenue from them, or even to ascertain how far they can be brought to contribute towards the exigencies of Government without discouragement to cultivation and industry. We have no data to go by; no established system to guide us; for caprice and rapacity were the sole springs which actuated the measures of our predecessor, under whose misrule personal safety and property were alike insecure.

Should new wants excite the industry of the Kandians to supply them, the many valuable natural productions of the country will amply furnish the means. The interior, it is well known, abounds with precious stones, and rich veins of metals may be concealed within its bosom; but till Government

send

send mineralogists and chemists, to explore and analize its hidden treasures, your inquiry on this point must remain unanswered. There probably never was a country so long, in part, occupied by Europeans as this has been, whose various productions were so imperfectly known, and so slightly investigated, for want of scientific men. Our neighbours the French have adopted a different plan in this respect, which we ought to follow.

It cannot escape the most careless observer, that the Kandian provinces offer many sources for commerce. Coffee and pepper grow wild: the former collected in the province of Ouwah is equal if not superior to Mocha coffee. I should think that this plant (from the luxuriance with which it grows) is indigenous to the island. The Portuguese or Dutch cannot be supposed to have carried these plants or seeds with them in their incursions upon the Kandian territories, much

less

less that they should have conveyed them into the Ouwah province, which was more distant than any other from former European settlements, and less obnoxious to invasion. Nor is it probable that the Kandians should have collected the plant or berry when their armies approached the sea coast. Ribiera, Baldius, or Valentyn, who are so minute in their description of Ceylon, would have noticed the introduction of the coffee tree, had it been, as at Java, imported. It is very certain that, at present, the shrub grows wild, and is loaded with berries. Should it be brought into regular cultivation, it would not require twenty years to draw the greater part of the Java coffee trade to Ceylon. Cotton and indigo plantations might also be established to any extent, as both plants grow extremely well, particularly the former, and the cultivation of rice in the interior already exceeds the consumption of its inhabitants, and might be rendered considerably more productive by transplantation, a mode of cultivation which prevails in every part of India, except Ceylon. I have no doubt that, in two or three years, the newly conquered provinces will supply us with the greater part of the rice we now are obliged to purchase from the continent of India, and with rice of superior and more nutritive quality.

The returns from the interior state that all the rice lands, which have remained uncultivated for several years past, are this season sown again, and promise an abundant harvest. New industry seems to animate every inhabitant. They are now convinced that the labour they bestow on the cultivation of their lands is for their own advantage, and that no Adikar, Dessave, or headman, can at his will and pleasure despoil them of the fruits of their labour.

It is most pleasing to observe how the confidence of these natives daily augments

augments towards our excellent General; they call him their father, and truly what father could listen with more benevolence to the grievances of his children than he does to their's! Let the complainant be rich or poor, he is heard with equal kindness; his case is inquired into by the General himself, and where assistance is necessary it is given immediately. No petition remains unanswered for many days. This is so well known, that few or no subjects for complaint arise; certainly none of a serious nature have come before the Governor, which is the more astonishing, if we consider what a system of oppression has prevailed for so many centuries in the Kandian country.

These provinces have now been for more than eighteen months in our possession, and during all this time not one act of violence has been committed by the natives, who have just emerged from such a state of abject barbarism and slavery as cannot be described, and who are now enjoying, for the first time, the blessing of freedom and security. On a late tour of his Excellency the Governor through the interior, a court of justice was held by him at Kandy, at which he presided in person. It was the first which it was found necessary to hold in fourteen months. The cases brought before the court generally arose from disputed title deeds, &c. &c., and were promptly decided according to the Kandian laws · neither party was obliged to pay enormous fees to proctors and other law advisers, and the party who failed of success had not to regret two losses at the same time.

The great road from Columbo to Kandy is nearly finished, under the superintendance of Captain King, of the Royal Staff corps, and aide-de-camp to the Governor, and will be passable for wheel carriages, except over the Balani mountain; but it is intended

intended to avoid that pass, by a circuitous route. From Kandy to Trincomalee the road is very excellent. It begins to be thinly inhabited, after having passed the Matale province, owing to the low lands abounding in swamps, the exhalations of which render it very unhealthy even for the natives. It was by this road that the Portuguese and Dutch brought to Kandy their cannons of a heavy calibre, of which we found a number buried under ground at the King's elephant stable. The post goes now from Columbo, viâ Kandy, to Trincomalee, in five days; the old road requires nine days.

Kandy is becoming a gay town, and several ladies have joined their husbands, who are either in garrison there or hold civil situations, and so healthy is it considered, that no officer has left it from choice since we took possession of the country!

Before I bid adieu to the Kandian provinces I must inform you, that the conquest and annexation to the crown of Great Britain of this fine and fertile country, the beauty, the salubrity, and the rich and various productions of which have given rise to the idea of its being the seat of Paradise, have cost not more, including every incidental expence, than £40,000. Its value, in every point of view, is most promising; but must, in a great measure, depend upon the means employed for its improvement. A considerable stimulus to the exertions of the natives has, as I have before observed, been already given, by the certainty the cultivator feels, under our dominion, that he who sows will reap; but to render the island flourishing and prosperous to the full extent of its resources, much is yet wanting, both in the old and in the new provinces. We are deplorably deficient in four essential articles; capital, a spirit of of enterprize, industry, and labourers; till we are supplied with these much must be be left undone. Capital will be drawn into action by confidence in government, and its successful employment will gradually give rise to a spirit of enterprize which, even in our old provinces, has degenerated under the discouragements of a depreciated coinage and exchange. The indolence of the Cingalese it will be most difficult to overcome; but inveterate as it is, it may not be insurmountable. They want the stimulus of example, and no remedy seems better calculated, in my opinion, to supply it, or to add to the deficiency of its stock, than the introduction of some thousand Chinese as colonists. The Chinese are a laborious, skilful and peaceable race of men, and easy to be obtained. I am aware that an unsuccessful attempt of the kind was made some years ago by government. It did not succeed for very obvious reasons. The im-

 portation

portation was not made from any part of China but from Prince of Wales' Island, where almost every Chinaman acquires bad habits from the company he associates with; that island being the Botany Bay of the East. These depraved Chinamen, when landed, were left to themselves; idleness and all the vices in its train became prevalent amongst them, and the scheme was abandoned. Are we never to make the experiment again, because it has once failed? The Chinese ought to be brought to Ceylon as they are to Java, direct from China, and then ruled by similar laws to those in force at Java. The advantages which government and the whole island would derive, from such an importation of industrious men, are incalculable; it is certainly owing to them that Java is at present one of the richest and best cultivated islands in the world.

The

The introduction of Chinamen into Ceylon, is of so much interest, that you will allow me to add a few more words on this subject, to which I have given every consideration, during a residence of sixteen months in Java, and nearly the whole of the Eastern Islands, to which places I was sent in 1813 and 1814, on a mission from his Majesty's government to Ceylon.

Every person, on landing in any part of Java, must be struck with the industrious habits of the numerous class of Chinese inhabitants, which offer the greatest contrasts to the indolent and lazy habits of the Dutch and Javanese. I landed in the middle of a very warm day at Batavia. Not an European was to be seen out of doors, except some of our young officers driving in open carriages from one shop to another. Mynheer was cooped up in his house, dressed in a loose night-gown, smoking his pipe, or dosing over it. The Javan lay stretched under

under a shady verandah on a mat, fast asleep: but the Chinese were hard at work in the smiths' or carpenters' work-sheds, or anxiously looking for customers at their shop doors: others groaned under heavy loads of goods, which they hawked about for sale; or were cheerfully working in the gardens and fields, and their crops showed that they had not been raised by slaves: they were not only abundant but neat.

The Chinese are the best gardeners and husbandmen which can be found; particularly if they once become possessed of any property: then their industry rises and displays itself in its brightest colours. There is not a trade with which they are not well acquainted. They build excellent carriages. They are masons, carpenters, wheelrights, smiths, painters, tanners, shoemakers, sadlers, taylors, confectioners, butchers, cooks, fishermen, distillers; in short, point out to them the means of gaining a livelihood, and

and they will soon acquire and excel in them.

I lived for two months at the country house of the China Major at Grisse, a sea-port on the eastern side of Java, and had a daily opportunity of conversing with this very intelligent man, who is possessed of considerable property in Java. Our conversation often turned on the measure of bringing China settlers to Ceylon, and he gave me his opinion very freely. I must reserve some of his observations for another time, because Java has since changed masters.

The result of my inquiries and observations on this subject are, that Chinamen can be imported into Ceylon direct from China, at an expence of about 110 or 120 Spanish dollars per head. I should think that the island of Solo (situated almost in the China sea, ninety miles west from Samboaugen, in the island of Mindanao, one of of the Philippines, where I resided for some time) with a good harbour, would be the most eligible place for fixing a resident, who could select, from the many China junks which touch there, the number of men required. The money thus laid out might be reimbursed by instalments, from the men so imported, as it is necessary for them to enter into a contract either with government or individuals for that purpose, on their being engaged. On the first establishment of such a colony in Ceylon, I would recommend that government alone should take the management of them, under certain rules which are absolutely necessary for their controul. It would be advisable to engage some respectable Chinamen of known industrious habits, if possessed of some little property the better; these men should be appointed China majors, or captains or lieutenants, as is the case in Java, and in them the civil jurisdiction

tion over their countrymen must, in some measure, be vested, and they must be allowed to exercise that sort of discipline over them, which their early habits and customs render necessary; they also should be empowered to collect the instalment agreed on, and afterwards any taxes which may be levied. By investing these superintendants with ostensible power over their countrymen, they become a most useful engine in the hands of government; for their inherent wish to rule (or to have show of ruling, the consequence of vanity) will make them faithful observers of the regulations laid down for their guidance, while the Chinamen will more cheerfully and readily obey such a superior than a foreigner.

It is well understood that it is not the best class of Chinamen who emigrate; therefore those who do so, it may be supposed, require in the beginning some coercion to keep them to their labour, and the power

power of slight punishment must be given to their superiors, without the interference of Europeans, except when it is abused. The Chinaman is naturally not cruel, and he begins early to aspire to the possession of property of his own, which, if once acquired, will soon render him eminently industrious.

The Chinese should be kept together, in colonies of two or three hundred, for the first few years, till they begin to acquire property, and government should go to the expence of allowing a certain number of female Chinese, which need not to be very great, as they intermarry with other women, the natives of the country in which they settle.

It would be necessary to set apart proper grounds for these new settlements, to build houses on them, to supply farming utensils, live stock and seeds. All this should be done before they arrive, that their useful labour

labour may immediately begin, that they should not have leisure for bad habits or connections, and that they the sooner should enjoy the sweets of their own labour, which is the greatest incitement to industry.

Small grants of land should be made to the most industrious, receiving from them part of the produce in lieu of rent. Their headmen should have similar grants of land on a more extended scale, and the more those are distinguished and rewarded, that are found deserving, the better the new colony will thrive.

It would require more time than I have at present, to enumerate the whole arrangement for bringing these settlers to Ceylon, or for their encouragement and government when there; but every person who has the welfare of this island at heart, should exert himself to promote the success of this plan; for, by the proper introduction

tion of Chinamen, and the application of their skill and industry, our coffee, indigo, and cotton plantations, would be brought to perfection, and the cultivation of rice be so extended, as to make that island, in a few years, the most valuable colony in the world.

The industry of the Chinese has never appeared to me in a more striking light than at Java, in the districts of Prabolingo and Besooki, situated in the eastern part of that island. These extensive tracks of land, forming a great province, were, a few years ago, sold by Governor Daendels to a Chinese family, whose head received the rank of China Major, for one million Spanish dollars. The whole was, when purchased, almost barren. At the time I saw it in 1813, the richest rice fields and sugar plantations and numerous villages presented themselves every where to your view. Aqueducts of several miles in length crossed the plains

for

for the better irrigation of the lands, and many thousand families lived and flourished, where, a short time before, scarcely a wild buffalo could have been fed.

At other places, such as Amboyna, Banda, Solo, Malacca, and Prince of Wales' Island, I found Chinamen in great numbers, and they constituted, every where, the most industrious and peaceable class of inhabitants.

If His Majesty's Government should be induced to make a fresh trial at Ceylon to introduce Chinamen, it is to be hoped that their treatment will be different from what it was when the first experiments were made. It will require much attention so far to attach them to Ceylon, as to induce them to come there in their own vessels, which they certainly might do, either from Acheen Head or Bencoolen, where their junks already resort: still when we advert to the many articles with which Ceylon supplies China,

 indirectly,

indirectly, and those which, if known to them, might be added to their wants, it is reasonable to presume, that when the intercourse between the two countries has been once established by the first colonists, it may be increased most beneficially. It would be lengthening a topic, on which I fear you will already think I have dwelt too long, to enumerate all the advantages of such an intercourse; I will only mention a direct sale of our seed pearls, cinnamon, ivory, satin-wood, shark's fins, &c. &c. which now reach them by a circuitous trade the emoluments of which are so much lost to the island.

Your next question, as to "the practicability, means, and policy of converting the natives of this island," to be fully answered, would require a volume, and more knowledge of the subject than I possess. That it is perfectly practicable, is past a doubt, from the numerous converts to christianity,

and

and their descendants, actually existing in Ceylon. Nearly all the Moodeliars and other headmen, employed by the British Government in our old territories profess the Protestant religion, and bring up their children in its tenets, and a large proportion of the inhabitants follow the example of their superiors. The Roman Catholics are still more numerous.

There is no part of India where Christianity has been so long established, and so well received as it is here. It is indeed the only colony in the East where, till lately, the attempt to propagate it has been made in a judicious and effectual manner; I mean by the slow but sure influence of education; by early inculcating its precepts, and at the same time enlightening the young mind, so as to enable it, at an age most susceptible of religious impressions, to distinguish truth from error. The grosser the error, the more absurd the system to be corrected, the greater the chance of success in supplanting it, by a more rational doctrine; and, perhaps, with the single exception of the homage paid to the intriguing deities of Greece and Rome, there never was a mode of worship more monstrous or absurd than that of Budhism, which prevails here. The introduction of Christianity in this island is coeval with the partial conquest of it by the Portuguese. They instituted schools in almost every village, for the instruction of the inhabitants in their religion and language. The latter continues to be generally spoken, in our old territories, and the knowledge of it by the natives materially assists the unwearied efforts of the Catholic priests sent from Goa, to preserve the influence of the Romish church, and to make proselytes. The pageantry of the Roman Catholic ceremonies is a powerful auxiliary to their zeal, and renders its exertions so effectual and so much beyond what our clergy

clergy or missionaries can accomplish, that it may admit of a question, whether we have not carried the liberal spirit of toleration beyond its proper boundary, by withdrawing those checks which the Dutch had established, to prevent this gaudy form of worship from gaining the ascendancy over the simpler ceremonials of Calvinism.

The influence of the Popish clergy over their flocks is unbounded, and they drain the country of considerable sums annually, for their support, levied for the most part on the poorer classes. These contributions are not under the control of our Government, and their exact amount is not ascertainable; but it may be guessed at, from the frequent arrivals of new priests to succeed the old ones, who return hence *gravis ære.* We should never forget, that if Ceylon were to be attacked by an European power, it would in all probability be by a Popish state, and that in such an event there might be a bias in the native Catholics to that potentate professing the same faith with themselves, which, if their numbers increased as rapidly as they have lately done, might not be perfectly consistent with our security.

The Dutch followed the steps of the Portuguese, and kept up the village schools. Their clergy, far more numerous than our own, regularly visited these establishments, examined the children in the Catechism, Belief, and Lord's Prayer, and preached to them in their own language. It was common for the principal Dutch families to stand sponsors for the children of the natives, who were named after them; and the Dutch government made it a rule to employ no native, even in the most subordinate situations, who could not produce his certificate of baptism. Some merely nominal christians, no doubt, by this plan, increased the apparent number of converts; but the majority of those who were in the

Dutch

Dutch service, when we conquered their possessions, and especially those of the higher orders, cultivated their new faith with sincerity and devotion.

Under the benevolent government of Mr. North, a school was formed for educating the sons of the principal natives, and instructing them in the English language. Two of these youths, who received the elements of their education at this seminary, are now in England, completing their studies at the expense of the British Government, the one for the bar, and the other for the church. The schools in the several villages are placed under the superintendance and direction of one of the British chaplains.

We have in one respect departed from the system of our predecessors. They taught their own languages in all the schools. It is only at the principal seminary at Hulfsdorp that English is taught. If natives were educated at this place, for the purpose of becoming teachers at the several village schools, it would be the means of gradually abolishing the use of the Portuguese language, now so prevalent; it would, in a great degree, diminish the influence of the Catholic priesthood, and it would increase the attachment of the natives to the British Government and religion.

There is another mean of promoting these objects which seems to me important. While great pains have been taken to enlighten the male part of our native subjects, the females, till very lately, have been left totally uninstructed. There was no school for girls of any description, till Lady Brownrigg established one for those of the Malabar cast, in the suburbs of Columbo, conducted under her ladyship's immediate superintendance. The children are educated by a native clergyman, and regularly attend divine

divine service at the Malabar Christian church, which has been recently erected, in the vicinity of Columbo, by the present Governor, and is regularly consecrated. It may be hoped that the same zeal, whioh has founded this establishment will be extended to the female offspring of Cingalese parents, who are equally in need of instruction.

Several Missionaries, from England, are assiduously applying themselves to the study of the Cingalese and Malabar languages, to enable them more effectually to extend their pious labours. A translation of the New Testament into the Pali and Cingalese languages, made by Mr. William Tolfrey, one of the civil servants, who has acquired a profound knowledge of both these dialects, is now in considerable forwardness, and a Bible society has been established in Columbo under the auspices of the government.

ment. Nor is that wanting, which is eminently calculated to ensure the success of those endeavours to extend the blessing of our religion—the influence of good example. Our excellent Governor with his family regularly attends divine service, and his humane and just conduct and extensive charity is a practical commentary which renders his observance of the Sabbath eminently useful. New chapels have been lately erected and our ecclesiastical establishment enlarged. Some Missionaries from America have reached Ceylon, but how far it may be prudent or necessary to encourage their visits may be reasonably doubted.

As to your question of policy when generally applied to the spreading of Christianity in this island, it admits but of one short answer, that no policy can be just, or ought to be attended to, which interferes with

with that paramount duty we owe to the Supreme Being, in whose hands we may be the humble instruments of spreading his sacred word, but not of circumscribing or counteracting its propagation. Farewell, and believe me, &c.

LETTER IV.

Begun at Sea and finished in London,
3d March, 1817.

DEAR SIR,

I WILL endeavour to answer your several questions which remained unanswered in my last letter.

While our vigilant Governor is adding to the revenues of the island on the one hand, he is indefatigably employed in reducing its expenditure on the other. The strictest economy has prevailed in every department since Sir Robert Brownrigg's administration. It would lead into too wide a field of detail, were I to notice every retrenchment which has been made. I will confine myself to a few of the more prominent instances, which, as affecting my own profession have come more immediately under

my

my observation. Reductions, to a certain extent, have taken place in all the military departments; the offices of military paymaster-general and auditor-general are abolished, and their duties are transferred to the civil auditors and paymasters-general; several officers on the staff here, such as the town-majors of Columbo and Trincomalee, the major of brigade in the island, &c. &c. have joined their regiments, and the officers on the personal staff do duty on the general staff. The Governor's actual receipts are reduced to much less than those of the Governors of the Cape of Good Hope, of St. Helena, or the Isle of France, who are paid in sterling money of Great Britain, and scarcely exceeds the salary of the chief justice of Ceylon, which is also paid at par, while the Governor, and every other public functionary on the island, civil or military (except the judges), receive their pay at a depreciated exchange. The disin-

terested

terested acquiescence of the Governor to these reductions had its influence on the ready submission of those who have been the objects of retrenchment.

In August 1812 the extra allowances for medical officers, which had been very profuse, were done away, and the hospitals placed on that footing which is laid down in his Majesty's regulations: the consequence has been a yearly saving of some thousand pounds sterling, whilst the sick have been equally well treated and attended. The gentlemen who were affected by the retrenchment received at the same period an increase of island allowances, which brings those of surgeons much above captains, and those of an assistant-surgeon above a subaltern's, to which two ranks they belong.

I will trespass upon your patience to state another instance of reduction of a charge, similar

similar in principle to the former, because it strikingly shews how much government miscalculates in commuting actual disbursements by gross allowances. The officer in charge of the barrack furniture was paid a round sum quarterly, for the repairs of the soldiers' cots; the Governor abolished this allowance, and the cots are now kept in repair at one-twentieth of the expence previously incurred.

There is another reduction of a more public nature too important to pass over, for it is one of the many beneficial results of our late military operations. The conquest of Kandy was scarcely achieved, when Sir Robert Brownrigg considered our power so well established in this island, that he reduced our small military force, and placed the 4th Ceylon regiment upon the half-pay, as he had been ordered to do from home, before Ministers knew of a

Kandian

Kandian war. Thus has a large tract of country been subdued and annexed to the British crown, not only without any augmentation of force, but its very acquisition has been the cause of considerably lessening the military establishment of the colony, without affecting its security otherwise than by giving it additional strength. Where can a similar instance be shown? Indeed, where was ever the acquisition of dominion so promoted and consolidated as this has been, by the mere influence of an honourable, just, and virtuous character on the feelings of a whole nation?

These reductions have nearly equalized the revenue and the expenditure of the island, each of which amounts to from £300,000 to £350,000 annually. The principal branches of the revenue and their products are as follow:

Cinnamon	£104,000
Custom House Duties	60,000
Land Rents, including Stamp Duties and Fines	56,000
Salt	24,000
Fish Rents, &c. and Licences	35,000
Chanks, Choy Root, Shark Fins, fine Woods, and lesser Articles	25,000
Post Office, &c.	5,000
	£230,000

You will observe that this statement does not include the receipts of the pearl fishery, which cannot be estimated from its uncertain produce and occurrence, and that it is also exclusive of our expectations from the new provinces. The civil and military expenditure have been nearly equal hitherto; but the recent reduction of the 4th native regiment will diminish the proportion for the military, while that of the civil department is rather augmented by the number of civil employments being necessarily increased by our recent acquisitions, and by the few retirements from that service which have lately taken place.

In the estimate of the civil department is comprehended the judicial establishment, the expence of which, including contingent charges, amounts to about £20,000 per annum. Whether so large an expenditure for the administration of justice in this colony be necessary, has been questioned by many more capable of forming an opinion upon such a subject than a military man may be supposed to be.

It may, however, be observed, that at Bombay, a Recorder's court, with a single judge to preside over it, at a salary of £5,000 a year, is found to be sufficient to dispense civil and criminal justice to a settlement and its dependencies, which for population, wealth, and commercial importance, as far surpasses that part of our

little

little colony to which alone the jurisdiction of the Supreme Court extends, as Rome does Mantua.

We have no manufactories in this island, for such I cannot call the making of a few pieces of cotton cloth, or some dozen coarse towels; nor is it likely that the little capital we have will be employed in such speculations, till we become more independent of the coast for the means of existence. Rice is imported yearly to the amount of from 200,000 or 250,000 bags, each weighing 164 pounds; the price paid per bag cannot be correctly stated, as i varies every year from 8 to 14 rix-dollars, and at one time rose even higher; but it has not been lower than 8 for the last five years; a medium price, 11 rix-dollars, for 225,000 bags of rice, gives £190,000. The payment for this rice carries away most of our money, and leaves the inhabitants without the means of establishing or cul-

 tivating

tivating cotton plantations. The cotton plant grows here in the highest perfection, and the money paid yearly to the coast merchant, for cotton cloth, amounts to from 6 to 800,000 rix-dollars, or about £60,000.

Rice and cotton cloth are the two chief articles of import, and are indispensable to the existence and comfort of the natives; other goods imported are too numerous to be detailed in a letter, but consist chiefly in articles of luxury, and may be valued at about from 80 to 100,000 pounds sterling. I calculate the Ceylon rix-dollar, or elephant rupee, at thirteen to one pound sterling, which is the medium price at which the government bills have sold for several years past. The real value of this coin in exchange, as fixed by government, is $11\frac{3}{7}$ to a pound sterling, or within a fraction $4\frac{1}{2}$ to a star pagoda. I have estimated the imports, receipts and expenditure at 13, and

and shall estimate the exports at the same rate, as it will save you the rather intricate calculation of rix-dollars, Star and Porto Novo pagodas, Sicca and Arcot rupees, new and old rate of exchange, or rate at which part of the pay is issued to civil and military officers; all which expressions for coin you will find every moment in a Ceylon account, the disadvantage of which is too obvious to require any comments here.

Our staple commodity is cinnamon, the sale of which is exclusively in the hands of Government; after the collection has been made, the cinnamon is sorted, and the best reserved for the Hon. East-India Company, who pay yearly £100,000 for all the fine cinnamon; the remainder is sold by government for the markets of India, under the proviso that it is not to be exported to Europe; its produce may be estimated at from 3 to £4,000 annually. Arrack ranks next in

 importance;

importance; about 5 or 6000 leagers, at 95 rix-dollars per leager, are yearly exported, which give about £40,000; tobacco (also in the hands of government) yields £20,000; coir (a rope used for cables and other purposes on board a ship, and made of the cocoa-nut husk) about £10,000; areka nuts 18 or £20,000; cocoa-nuts and oil about 5 or £6,000; chanks about 6 or £8,000; coffee, pepper, jaggery, salt fish, wood in planks and blocks, &c. &c. may amount to about 25 or £30,000. This calculation is made in round sums; and as I had not the means of extracting it from the Custom-House books, some errors may have crept into my statement, but I am certain that they are not very material, as I gained my information from some of the best informed gentlemen in the civil service. The result of this statement is very unfavourable to Ceylon, as it gives a balance of trade of more than £100,000

£100,000 against the island, as you will see from the following statement.

Imports.		Exports.	
Rice	£190,000	Cinnamon	£104,000
Cotton cloth	60,000	Arrack	40,000
Articles of luxury, &c. &c, ...	100,000	Tobacco..........	20,000
		Coir	10,000
		Areka............	19,000
		Cocoa-nuts and Oil	6,000
		Chanks	7,000
		Coffee, Pepper, &c. &c.............	27,000
	£350,000		£233,000

Balance against Ceylon £117,000. Whilst this balance exists it will be in vain to expect that the exchange should become more favourable. Indeed it is likely, for a time, to be worse rather than better: for the late reduction of our military force has deprived us of the means of remittance, supplied by drawing on the Treasury for the pay of the suppressed regiment, and thus by lessening the amount of government

 bills

bills (and we have no other) has raised their value. This depreciated exchange is the bane of our prosperity. It lessens the value of what we receive, whilst it enhances the price of all we have to purchase. Government as well as individuals suffer under its influence on what is paid for every article of foreign supply.

The population of Ceylon is not ascertained, a regular census never having taken place; but, I believe that government is preparing for that measure, which is subject to very great difficulties, on account of the dispersed state in which the natives live, and the facility with which, from the few moveables they possess, they remove from one district to another; but the information I have been able to collect gives me reason to think that the whole island may have a population of one million six hundred thousand souls, of all sexes and ages, and including all classes of people, such as Cingalese,

galese, Malabars, Moormen, Hindoos, Malays, Portuguese and Dutch.

The Cingalese, which includes the Kandians (although Cordiner and Perceval speak of them as two different races of people) are the most numerous, and certainly not the most industrious part of the population. I am not aware of any other difference between the Kandians and Cingalese than that the former generally allow their beards to grow. They have the same language, religion, customs, and features, and are alike great observers of distinctions of rank. The next and by far most industrious class of natives are the Moormen, dispersed over the whole island. The Hindoos and Malabars live in particular in the eastern and northern districts.

The Malays are not numerous, and do not deserve to be called treacherous, revengeful or addicted to thieving. I have, by several years experience and close obser-

vation

vation of those under my immediate command, found them a faithful, obedient and brave race of people; the same character is given to them by all our officers here as well as those who have been for some years in Java. That the cruel and barbarous manner in which the Dutch have generally treated them, has at times produced sudden fits of madness, in which they seek their death by attempting to murder indiscriminately every human being they encounter, is undeniable; but how does it happen that acts of violence have not occurred either in Ceylon, at the Cape, or Java, since we have been in possession of these Colonies? For this reason, that our laws protect every person from oppression. With regard to their alleged propensity to thieving, I can only refer you to the Civil and Military Judicial Records, where it will be found that other natives and even Europeans are at least as often guilty of the same crime as the

the Malays. I consider the Malays the best native soldiers we have. They are a hardy, bold and brave race of men, and much attached to their officers. Their bravery, they have shown by their resistance and by the slaughter they occasioned amongst our troops at the taking of Java. The yearly casualty returns of the 1st Ceylon regiment, composed entirely of Malays,* shew that they are a hardy race of men, and detest being in hospitals. They have another great advantage over the other native troops of India, they have fewer prejudices. In fact, when properly treated by their officers, they have none. They relinquish, without murmuring, even when in garrison, their native holidays; they eat meat, if rice is not to be had in sufficient quantity, and certainly do not require opium. I know that for four months a party of Malay recruits

* See the second letter, page 67.

cruits for the 1st Ceylon regiment (54 in number) was on board his Majesty's frigate the Malacca, and their quiet, orderly, and good conduct, obtained the approbation of Captain D. Mackay, R. N. and all the officers of that ship, with the good-will of the men, who often joined their pork messes to the rice and curry of salt fish of the Malays.

The descendants of the Portuguese and Dutch inhabitants are few in number, and most of them, by frequent intermarriage with native women, are black or copper coloured. They are generally employed as clerks in the different offices, where most of them are useful individuals, and know, by attention to their duty, how to gain the good will of their superiors.

The slaves in this island amount to about 7000; they are well treated by their masters and lead a very easy life, the greater part of them being employed as house servants, carpenters,

penters, masons, &c. One of the best and most humane arrangements which has lately taken place, has been effected by Sir Alexander Johnston's influence over the owners of these slaves. They have, at his suggestion, come to a resolution to declare, by a public act, that all children born of their slaves from the 12th of August, 1816, being the birth day of his Royal Highness the Prince Regent, shall be free. A noble manner of celebrating that day.

Your account of the opinions entertained in England, as coming from persons who ought to be acquainted with India and particularly with Ceylon, respecting our campaign, is amusing enough. It is entertaining, with this rich and beautiful country in our hands, and annexed by the suffrage of the natives, to the crown of Great Britain, to learn the speculation of politicians at home, on the impossibility of conquering Kandy; on the lives we should sacrifice; and

and on the enormous expence we should incur by the rash and vain attempt. How fortunate that we were placed beyond the reach of their advice, or the terror of their predictions! The judgment of these gentlemen (from this specimen) cannot be very sound, and I hope, if it has any influence in public affairs in future, that their opinion will not be always implicitly taken and followed, concerning Ceylon; at least so long as it remains under the government of General Sir Robert Brownrigg, whose merits and resources they are not able to appreciate. Now that these foreboders of evil have turned out to be false prophets, and that the war which they had deprecated as certain of failure, and teeming with calamity, has been completely successful, unattended by a single disastrous event, it seems other, and more formidable criticks have succeeded them, who seek, in the very triumph of our arms, for a subject of censure.

sure. The tyrant whom we have subdued and deposed, who pitied no one, becomes an object of their tender interest. "We had no right (they tell us) to call hereditary legitimate sovereigns to account for their misconduct (a gentle word as applied to the acts of their *protégé*), nor to dethrone them for maltreating their own subjects, nor to judge them upon our principles of society. Such an interference is trenching upon the independence of rightful sovereigns and violating the universal principles of political society." To this heavy charge the answer is not difficult. It does not altogether apply to the King of Kandy, nor to our relation with him. He is not a legitimate hereditary monarch. He was an usurper placed on the Kandian throne by the intrigues of an artful minister (Adikar) who thought to rule in his name; but who, after a time, fell a victim to his tyranny. He (Rajah Wikrime Singa) was a foreigner from

from the coast of Malabar, of a race long detested by the Cingalese. We were not provoked to hostility against him by his conduct towards his own subjects, nor did we attempt to avail ourselves of the odium its despotism had excited in them, to avenge the massacre of our sick and disarmed soldiers at Kandy in 1803. For twelve years he was suffered to exult with impunity in the success of this signal act of treachery and cruelty against our government, and to spread terror and oppression through his usurped dominions. When another of his Prime Ministers (whose wife and children he had butchered) then the chief of one of his principal provinces, which with several others were in revolt, fled to Columbo, and sought our co-operation, we gave him our protection, but denied our assistance, and this protection was afforded from the dictates of humanity alone, and with every precaution which could prevent its giving umbrage to his savage master. It

was

was not till this monster renewed his barbarity on British subjects; till he had seized and mutilated the peaceable inhabitants of our frontiers, who had given no cause of offence; till he made an irruption into our territories with an armed force, that we waged war against him and him alone, for the aggravated outrages and injuries by which he had long incurred the just resentment of the British nation—" to secure the permanent tranquillity of the British settlements in Ceylon, which had become incompatible with his avowed and inveterate enmity, and to vindicate the honour of the British name." It is true that we availed ourselves of the detestation in which his character was universally held by the Kandians, and of their impatience under his misrule, to render successful those hostilities which he had made unavoidable, and the success of which was no less necessary to their security than to our own. It is also true that in the declaration of war we noticed "their supplication to be delivered from their oppressions, and to subvert that Malabar dominion, which, during three generations, had tyrannized over the country;" but these were subordinate and auxiliary grounds, and, as I have before shown, not the essential causes of warfare—not those for which, exclusive of our own injuries and insults, war would have been resorted to.

A reference to the convention of the 2d of March, 1815, with which this war terminated, will make it evident that it was not a British viceroy who accused, sentenced, and punished the tyrant whose acts had provoked the war—who decided between him and his subjects, and cashiered him for the internal acts of his government. As far as relates to these acts, his accusation is made, and his sentence pronounced by the nation he had offended, re-

presented

presented by their chiefs and headmen, who signed the convention which states his enormities. It might as well be said that these Kandian chiefs decided between him and the British government, because they concurred in the punishment inflicted upon him for his misdeeds to both parties.

His accusation was manifested by the entire abandonment of his people before it was embodied in the convention, and the sentence which hurled him from the throne was hailed as their deliverance. A sentence not dictated by us alone, not founded upon principles of refinement distinct from the ruder state of the Kandians, but perfectly consistent with their own laws and usages, and prompted by those feelings which are common to the nature of man in every stage of civilization— feelings the result of outraged humanity, and dictated by the impulses of self-protection.

I trust you will agree with me, that the whole conduct of our upright governor in this transaction, is not only justifiable but highly commendable; that in deposing this execrated tyrant, he has violated no fundamental principle upon which the independence of sovereigns either in Europe or Asia rests. Had he sent an army to Japan to depose its monarch for tyrannizing over his people, it might have been said that the same plea would justify our attacking Spain for oppression to her patriot subjects, or for despoiling Africa of her slaves. Political morality no doubt is universal—the same in the east as in the west; but the cases involving any question respecting it, must be alike, before any argument can be founded upon a comparison of them.

It must be shown that England stands in the same relation to Spain, as the British settlement in Ceylon does to Kandy: this is the not the fact; they are not such near neighbours; the ocean divides them. Scotland before the union would have been a more applicable instance. Would any monarch of England, when Scotland was an independent kingdom, have suffered English troops, who had surrendered their arms under a capitulation, or when sick in a Scottish hospital, to have been butchered in cold blood? Would England have suffered its borders to have been passed, and the peaceable inhabitants of Northumberland mutilated and murdered without resenting the insult and outrage? Had there been an usurper on the Scottish throne at the time, the (instigator of these acts,) whose despotic cruelty had made him universally odious to his subjects, would an English monarch be said to have violated the law of nations in assisting them to expel him from the throne; or, with the assent of the nation, by annexing this adjoining country to his own dominions?

The contiguity of Scotland renders this supposed case more similar than that which has been adduced; but there is a real case still more in point, in the downfal of Tippoo Sahib, the imprisonment of his children, and the exclusion of his descendants from the throne of Mysore. He was an independent sovereign whose territories were adjacent to our own. He manifested that rancorous enmity to the India Company's government, which made the existence of his power incompatible with the permanency or security of our possessions: on these grounds he was attacked and defeated in the capital of his empire, killed in its defence, and his dominion transferred, nominally to the race of its ancient sovereigns, but actually to the East India Company.

It

It seems difficult, with any colour of consistency, to commend the just policy of this act of the Marquis Wellesley's government, and to condemn Sir Robert Brownrigg; yet this was a measure for which this enlightened statesman received the thanks of Parliament, and the general applause of the British nation. Not a voice was heard to arraign the proceeding on the ground of its violating the rights of sovereigns, or infringing in any way the great principles of political justice.

Here I will take leave of these cavillers, who like Milton's fallen angels strive

> "Out of good still to find means of evil,"

and conclude the subject by communicating to you the terms of high approbation in which our good and excellent General's conduct in this affair, has been noticed by those whom it is his proudest ambition to please.—(See Appendix.)

APPENDIX.

No. I.

PROCLAMATION

By His Excellency Lieutenant General ROBERT BROWNRIGG, *Governor and Commander in Chief in and over the British Settlements and Territories in the Island of Ceylon, with the Dependencies thereof,*

IN COUNCIL.

HIS Excellency the Governor and Commander in Chief of the British settlements in the island of Ceylon, could not hear with indifference the prayers of the inhabitants of five extensive provinces, constituting more than one half of the Kandian kingdom, who, with one unanimous voice raised against the tyranny and oppression of their ruler, taking up arms in defence of their lives, or flying from his power, implored the protection of the British government, while the most convincing circumstances indicated corresponding sentiments from the same causes in other provinces less within the reach of direct communication. Neither could his Excellency contemplate, without the liveliest emotions of indignation and resentment, the atrocious barbarity recently perpetrated in Kandy upon ten innocent subjects of the British government, seven

seven of whom instantly died of their sufferings, and three miserable victims were sent, in defiance, with their mutilated limbs, across the limits, to relate the distressing tale, and exhibit the horrid spectacle to the eyes of an insulted government, and an indignant people, in the capital of the British settlements.

In the perpetrator of these acts, his Excellency convincingly recognizes the true author of that implacable animosity which has constantly been opposed to every approach of friendly intercourse so often attempted on the part of his Majesty's government.

No shadow of doubt now remains that the rejection of all relations of amity originated and continues with the king alone, and that the people are no otherwise parties to such a policy, than as they are compelled to become so by a coercion alike hostile to the British interests, and intolerable to themselves.

To him and his advisers is imputable the impossibility, proved by repeated trials, of terminating, by any just or defined conditions, a state of relations unsettled and precarious beyond all precedent—which bears no essential character of a peace, nor has any title to that appellation—which yields no solid tranquillity, or safe intercourse, but perpetuates the alarms of war without its remedies—and which, to continue any longer after a public unequivocal act of hostility, would be to sanction injury and encourage insult.

By the irresistible influence of these feelings and considerations, his Excellency had become convinced of the unavoidable necessity of resolving to carry his Majesty's arms into the Kandian country. In this, however, he has been anticipated by the irruption of

an

an armed Kandian force into the British territory, who having pursued the fugitive inhabitants across the boundary river of Sitawaka, fired upon them from the opposite bank, and finally, crossing that river in arms into the Hewagam Korle, proceeded to commit depredations on his Majesty's subjects.

This measure therefore supersedes every deliberative consideration, and leaves no choice but that of repelling the hostile forces from the British frontier.

But it is not against the Kandian nation that the arms of his Majesty are directed; his Excellency proclaims hostility against that tyrannical power alone, which has provoked, by aggravated outrages and indignities, the just resentment of the British nation, which has cut off the most ancient and noble families in his kingdom, deluged the land with the blood of his subjects, and, by the violation of every religious and moral law, become an object of abhorrence to mankind.

For securing the permanent tranquillity of these settlements, and in vindication of the honour of the British name; for the deliverance of the Kandian people from their oppressions; in fine, for the subversion of that Malabar dominion which, during three generations, has tyrannized over the country, his Excellency has resolved to employ the powerful resources placed at his disposal.

His Excellency hereby proffers to every individual of the Kandian nation the benign protection of the British government; exhorts them to remain without fear in their dwellings, to regard the armed forces who pass through their villages as protectors and friends,

and

and to co-operate with them for the accomplishment of these beneficial objects.

In their march through the country the most rigorous discipline will be observed by the British troops; the peaceable inhabitants will be protected from all injury in their persons and property, and payment will scrupulously be made for every article of provisions which they furnish. Their religion shall be held sacred, and their temples respected. The power of his Majesty's arms will be exerted only against those, who, deserting the cause of their country, oppose the progress of his Majesty's troops, and of their own countrymen united in arms for their deliverance.

Lastly, His Excellency promises, in the name of his Majesty the King of Great Britain, to the chiefs, the continuance of their respective ranks and dignities; to the people, relief from all arbitrary severities and oppressions, with the fullest protection of their persons and property; and to all classes the inviolate maintenance of their religion, and the preservation of their ancient laws and institutions, with the extension of the blessings resulting from the establishment of justice, security, and peace, which are enjoyed by the mos favoured nations living under the safeguard of the British crown.

By order of the Council,

(Signed) JAMES GAY,

Sec. to Council.

No. II.

Head Quarters, Kandy, 2d March, 1815.

GENERAL ORDERS.

THE undermentioned Proclamation published by authority of his Excellency the Governor is here inserted for the general information of the army.

PROCLAMATION.

At a convention held on the second day of March, in the year of Christ 1815, and the Cingalese year 1736, at the palace in the city of Kandy, between his Excellency Lieutenant General Robert Brownrigg, Governor and Commander in Chief in and over the British settlements and territories in the island of Ceylon, acting in the name and on behalf of his Majesty George the Third King, and his Royal Highness George Prince of Wales, Regent of the United Kingdom of Great Britain and Ireland on the one part; and the Adikars, Desaves, and other principal chiefs of the Kandyan provinces, on behalf of the inhabitants: and in presence of the Mohottales, Coraals, Vidahns, and other subordinate headmen from the several provinces; and of the people then and there assembled on the other part, it is agreed and established as follows.

1st. That the cruelties and oppressions of the Malabar ruler, in the arbitrary and unjust infliction of bodily tortures, and the pains of death without trial, and sometimes without an accusation or the possibility of a crime, and in the general contempt and contravention of all civil rights, have become flagrant, enormous, and intolerable; the acts and maxims of his government

vernment being equally and entirely devoid of that justice which should secure the safety of his subjects, and of that good faith which might obtain a beneficial intercourse with the neighbouring settlements.

2d. That the Rajah Sri Wikreme Rajah Sinha, by the habitual violation of the chief and most sacred duties of a sovereign, has forfeited all claims to that title or the powers annexed to the same, and is declared fallen and deposed from the office of King.—His family and relatives, whether in the ascending, descending, or collateral line, and whether by affinity or blood, are also for ever excluded from the throne—and all claim and title of the Malabar race to the dominion of the Kandyan provinces is abolished and extinguished.

3d. That all male persons being or pretending to be relations of the late Rajah Sri Wikreme Rajah Sinha either by the affinity of blood, and whether in the ascending, descending, or collateral line, are hereby declared enemies to the government of the Kandyan provinces, and excluded and prohibited from entering those provinces on any pretence whatever, without a written permission for that purpose, by the authority of the British government, under the pains and penalties of martial law, which is hereby declared to be in force for that purpose; and all male persons of the Malabar cast, now expelled from the said provinces, are, under the same penalties, prohibited from returning, except with the permission before mentioned.

4th. The dominion of the Kandyan provinces is vested in the Sovereign of the British Empire, and to be exercised through the governors or lieutenant-governors

nors of Ceylon for the time being and their accredited agents, saving to the Adikars, Desaves, Mohottales, Coraals, Vidahns, and all other chief and subordinate native headmen, lawfully appointed by authority of the British government, the rights, privileges, and powers of their respective offices, and to all classes of the people the safety of their persons and property, with their civil rights and immunities, according to the laws, institutions, and customs established and in force amongst them.

5th. The religion of Budha, professed by the chiefs and inhabitants of these provinces is declared inviolable, and its rites, ministers, and places of worship are to be maintained and protected.

6th. Every species of bodily torture, and all mutilation of limb, member, or organ, are prohibited and abolished.

7th. No sentence of death can be carried into execution against any inhabitant, except by the written warrant of the British Governor, or Lieutenant-governor for the time being, founded on a report of the case made to him through the accredited agent or agents of the government, resident in the interior, in whose presence all trials for capital offences are to take place.

8th. Subject to these conditions, the administration of civil and criminal justice and police over the Kandyan inhabitants of the said provinces, is to be exercised according to established forms, and by the ordinary authorities, saving always the inherent right of government to redress grievances, and reform abuses, in all instances whatever, particular or general, where such interposition shall become necessary.

9th. Over

9th. Over all other persons, civil or military, residing or resorting to these provinces, not being Kandyans, civil and criminal justice, together with police, shall, until the pleasure of his Majesty's government in England may be otherwise declared, be administered in manner following.

1. All persons, not being commissioned or non-commissioned military officers, soldiers, or followers of the army, usually held liable to military discipline, shall be subject to the magistracy of the accredited agent or agents of the British government in all cases, except charges of murder, which shall be tried by special commissions, to be issued from time to time by the governor for that purpose. Provided always as to such charges of murder wherein any British subject may be defendant, who might be tried for the same by the laws of the United Kingdom of Great Britain and Ireland in force, for the trial of offences committed by British subjects, shall not be tried on any charge of murder, alleged to have been perpetrated in the Kandyan provinces, otherwise than by virtue of such laws of the United Kingdom.

2. Commissioned or non-commissioned military officers, soldiers, or followers of the army, usually held amenable to military discipline, shall, in all civil and criminal cases wherein they may be defendants, be liable to the laws, regulations, and customs of war, reserving to the Governor and Commander in Chief, in all cases falling under this ninth article, an unlimited right of review over every proceeding civil, or military, had by virtue thereof, and reserving also full power to make such particular provisions conformably

to

to the general spirit of the said article, as may be found necessary to carry its principles into full effect.

10th. Provided always that the operation of the several preceding clauses shall not be contravened by the provisions of any temporary or partial proclamation published during the advance of the army, which provisions, in so far as compatible with the said preceding articles, are hereby repealed.

11th. The royal dues and revenues of the Kandian provinces, are to be managed and collected for his Majesty's use, and the support of the provincial establishment, according to lawful custom, and under the direction and superintendance of the accredited agent or agents of the British government.

12th. His Excellency the Governor will adopt provisionally, and recommend to the confirmation of his Royal Highness the Prince Regent, in the name and on behalf of his Majesty, such dispositions in favour of the trade of these provinces, as may facilitate the export of their products, and improve the returns, whether in money, or in salt, clothes, or other commodities, useful and desirable to the inhabitants of the Kandian country.

GOD SAVE THE KING.

By his Excellency's Command,
(Signed) JAMES SUTHERLAND,
Deputy Secretary.

By the Lieutenant General's Command,
L. D. BUSSCHE,
Acting Deputy Adjutant General.

No. III.

Head Quarters, Columbo, 13th June, 1815.

GENERAL ORDERS.

The lamented death this day of Major William Willerman, Deputy Quarter Master General to the army serving in Ceylon, is a circumstance of such deep interest to that army, in being deprived of their most efficient staff-officer, connected with the high military reputation and professional abilities of the deceased; thus at an early period of his life lost to his King and country, as to entitle his memory to the honours due to superior rank: the flag of the fort of Columbo will therefore be hoisted, and remain half staff high during the day, and minute guns will be fired from the ramparts in the evening, as the body passes to the grave.

It must be left to an abler pen than the Commander of the Forces can boast, to eulogize in adequate terms an officer of Major Willerman's distinguished character, full of honour, talent, and military ardour. His has been a brilliant career, though in a comparatively subordinate rank. His eminent services in Flanders, Sicily, Portugal, Spain, and Holland, have been repeatedly honoured with the approbation of his Royal Highness the Duke of York, the Duke of Wellington, Sir Ralph Abercromby, and Sir John More, and the fruits of his labours, and the proofs of his superior topographical genius, will long remain in the military archives, memorials of his fame and acquirements. To Lieutenant General Brownrigg, who knew Major Willerman's man's worth for years past, whose companion in the field he has been in some trying scenes, who witnessed his bravery, admired his attainments, and reaped the advantage of his aid, to whom he justly attributes in a great degree the success which attended the late operations in the Kandian provinces; his is an afflicting task, now to have the melancholy duty devolve to him of recording thus feebly the merits of his dear departed friend. Distinguished as Major Willerman was professionally, so was he amiable in private society, where his urbanity and universality of talent, made him always an acceptable member; while deplored as his loss will be by his immediate connections, those friends who regarded him with affection, and his brother officers who held him in esteem—all will drop a tear of sympathy at the departure for a better world of a virtuous man, a brave soldier, and a polished gentleman; may the Almighty Disposer of all human events receive him in his holy kingdom.

All the troops in garrison off duty will attend the funeral of Major Willerman this afternoon, at an hour that will be made known.

By the Lieutenant General's command,

(Signed) L. D. BUSSCHE,

Acting Deputy Adjutant General.

No. IV.

Head Quarters, Columbo, 2d June, 1816.

GENERAL ORDERS.

The Commander of the Forces duly estimating as he does, the high and gracious approbation of his Royal Highness the Prince Regent, of the conduct of the troops employed in the Kandian campaign, as conveyed in Earl Bathurst's dispatch which was published in a gazette extraordinary yesterday—thinks it proper that this gratifying testimony of approbation, so honourable to the army serving in Ceylon, should appear in General Orders.

And as the same gazette contains a proclamation establishing, under the opinion of the law officers in England certain constructions of the act of convention passed in Kandy on the 2d of March, 1815;

And, amongst other things, declaring the administration of justice applicable to military persons serving in the interior, the whole gazette is here published for the information of the troops, and as a military record.

Columbo, 1st June, 1816.

The Governor has been honoured with a dispatch from the Right Honourable the Earl Bathurst, on the occasion of having laid before his Royal Highness the Prince Regent, his Excellency's official report of the successful issue of the Kandian expedition and the capture of the king.

By

By this communication his Excellency has had the heartfelt pleasure to receive, on the part of his Royal Highness, the most unqualified approbation of his conduct, throughout the whole of those proceedings.

He is at the same time charged to announce his Royal Highness's gracious acknowledgment of the meritorious services of the officers and soldiers who served under his Excellency's command, and particularly to express the sense which his Royal Highness entertains of the conduct and services of the honourable John D'Oyly, Esq.

This pleasing duty will be best fulfilled by publishing his Lordship's communication in his own words—nor can his Excellency consider that part of the dispatch, which more immediately relates to himself, as wholly inapplicable to those, who by sharing in the enterprise, are entitled to participate in the full measure of its most gratifying result.

Downing Street, 28th August, 1815.

SIR,

I have laid before his Royal Highness the Prince Regent your dispatch of the 25th of February, delivered to me by Major Brownrigg, in which you announce the invasion and conquest of the kingdom of Kandy, and the capture of the King and his adherents.

The success of your enterprise has been so complete and immediate, that you must have yourself anticipated the lively satisfaction with which his Royal Highness received the intelligence. Had it been confined to the mere liberation of a people from a foreign despotism (as sanguinary and cruel as that under which the inhabitants of Kandy so long groaned) it could not but have been grateful to the feelings of his Royal Highness: but as the overthrow of that tyranny has given increased security to his Majesty's possessions, and has been followed by an annexation of territory, voluntarily and unanimously made by its inhabitants, the satisfaction which his Royal Highness would in any case have felt, derives considerable accession from these circumstances, and from the proofs which they afford on the part of a whole people, of confidence in the British name and character.

His Royal Highness has commanded me to assure you that he considers this favourable result, as mainly to be attributed to the wise and judicious policy which you have uniformly adopted; to the promptitude with which, when war was unavoidable, you decided upon its immediate commencement, and to the vigour with which you planned and conducted its operations.

His Royal Highness has much pleasure in acknowledging the meritorious services of the officers and men under your command: and although the expedition could not, from the character of the enemy, and the resistance made by him, afford any opportunity for the display of their more splendid military qualities, his Royal Highness nevertheless considers them equally entitled to his approbation, for the fortitude with which they endured and overcame the peculiar difficulties of such a campaign, and for the excellent discipline uniformly maintained by them.

I am also commanded particularly to express the sense which his Royal Highness entertains of the conduct

duct and services of Mr. D'Oyly upon the late occasion.—To his intelligence in conducting the negociations, first with the Kandian government, and latterly with the Adikars and others who opposed it; to his indefatigable activity in procuring information, and in directing the military detachments, the complete success of the enterprize is principally owing; and his Royal Highness avails himself with pleasure of this opportunity of expressing how greatly he appreciates, not only Mr. D'Oyly's latter services, but those which he has at former periods, by his attention to the Kandian department, rendered to the colony and his country.

It only remains for me to convey to you the Prince Regent's entire approbation of your conduct throughout the whole of these proceedings, and his confident expectation that, under your guidance, the Kandian provinces will be so administered as to contribute to the prosperity and welfare of the inhabitants, and to the permanent security of his Majesty's possessions in the East.

I have the honour to be,

Sir,

Your most obedient humble servant,

(Signed) BATHURST.

Governor

SIR ROBERT BROWNRIGG, Bt. G. C. B.

&c. &c. &c.

PROCLAMATION

By his Excellency Lieutenant General Sir ROBERT BROWNRIGG, *Knight Grand Cross of the most Honourable Military Order of the Bath, Governor and Commander in Chief in and over the British Settlements and Territories in the island of Ceylon, with the Dependencies thereof.*

A dispatch, of which the following is a copy, having been received from the Right Honourable Lord Bathurst, one of his Majesty's principal Secretaries of State, respecting the convention concluded in Kandy, on the 2d of March, 1815, the said dispatch is published for general information.

Downing Street, 13th October, 1815.

SIR,

In my dispatch of the 30th of August, I informed you that I had referred to the consideration of his Majesty's law-servants, those articles of the convention for the settlement of the Kandian country, which had been the subject of discussion.

I have the now honour of transmitting to you a copy of their opinion, which is so full upon all the points submitted to their consideration, as to render it unnecessary for me to furnish you with instruction, beyond that of adhering to the principles which they have laid down; and in order to prevent any uncertainty, as to the liability of military persons in the Kandian country, to remain subject to the martial law, I am to acquaint you, that although his Royal Highness the Prince

Prince Regent has generally approved the convention by which that territory has become annexed to his Majesty's dominions: his Royal Highness has declined adopting the pre-existing laws and courts of Kandy, as forms of the King's civil judicature, until more detailed information shall have been obtained, as to the nature of these laws, and the changes which it may be expedient to introduce in their administration.

I have the honour to be,
Sir,
Your most obedient humble servant,
(Signed) BATHURST.

Governor
SIR ROBERT BROWNRIGG, Bt. G. C. B.
&c. &c. &c.

In conformity to the principles laid down in the opinion of the law officers of his Majesty's government in England, (to which principles the Governor is instructed to adhere), it is hereby declared and notified as follows: to wit.

1st. That the provision contained in the first section of the ninth or provisional article of the convention, respecting commissions to be issued by the Governor for the trial of charges of murder in certain specified cases, will cease to be in force from henceforth.

" 2ndly. That the ancient laws of Kandy are to be " administered till his Majesty's pleasure shall be " known as to their adoption *in toto*, as to all persons " within those provinces, or their partial adoption as " to the natives, and the substitution of new laws and " tribunals,

" tribunals, for the trial and punishment of his Ma-
" jesty's European subjects, for offences committed
" therein.

" 3dly. That persons committing those offences
" cannot be tried by the supreme court, as at present
" established for Ceylon, till the Kandian provinces
" are annexed to, or made dependencies of that set-
" tlement or government: but that British subjects
" may be proceeded against in England under the 33d
" Henry VIII. chap. 23d."

4thly. Concerning the 2d section of the said 9th or provisional article, that the same being, in substance, conformable to the provisions of the mutiny act and articles of war as applicable to the present state and condition of the Kandian country, will, until his Majesty shall otherwise provide, remain in force, and extend to " all persons who are commissioned, or in the
" pay of his Majesty as officers, or who are listed, or
" in pay as soldiers."

GOD SAVE THE KING.

Given at Columbo, the 31*st day of May*, 1816.

By command of his Excellency the Governor,

JOHN RODNEY,

Chief Secretary to Government.

To be published in the Kandian provinces,

By order of his Excellency the Governor,

JAMES SUTHERLAND,

Sec. Kandian Provinces.

By the Lieutenant General's Command,

(Signed) L. D. BUSSCHE,

Act. Dep. Adj. Gen.

No. V.

Head Quarters, Columbo, 15th June, 1816.

GENERAL ORDERS.

THE Commander of the Forces having this day been honoured with a dispatch from his Royal Highness the Commander in Chief, on the subject of the late Kandian expedition, the Lieutenant General cannot for a moment delay publishing the same to the army.

In participating with the troops which he had the honour to command on that service, the heartfelt satisfaction arising from this communication, the flattering and parental terms in which his Royal Highness the Commander in Chief has condescended to announce the gracious thanks and approbation of his Royal Highness the Prince Regent, as well as the favourable opinion, congratulations, and thanks expressed by his Royal Highness himself, on the conduct and result of the expedition, will no doubt be fully appreciated by the army.

The Commander of the Forces, overwhelmed as he really is with sentiments of grateful acknowledgment, for the honour of being enabled to convey such high and distinguished testimonials, presents them to the officers and soldiers as the reward most honourable to them, and best calculated to gratify military feeling.

Horse Guards, 16th October, 1815.

Sir,

I have duly received your letter of the 26th February last, and Major General Sir Henry Torrens has laid before me your dispatch of the previous date, enclosing your report upon the operations against the kingdom of Kandy.

Having laid these dispatches before the Prince Regent, I have great pleasure in obeying his Royal Highness's commands, by expressing to you his high sense and approbation of the able disposition you had adopted for the invasion of that country, and of the manner in which it was conducted towards the total overthrow of the enemy's power, and the annexation of his territory to the crown of Great Britain.

His Royal Highness remarked, that although the enterprise had not met with the opposition or loss in the field which the strength of the country, and the facilities for defence possessed by the enemy, had rendered probable, yet the obstacles opposed to its execution, could only have been overcome by the judicious arrangements adopted by you for conducting the operation, and by the intelligence, steady discipline, and good conduct of the officers and troops employed under your orders. His Royal Highness has therefore desired your acceptance of his thanks for your services upon this occasion, and that you will likewise convey them to the whole of the army employed in the subjugation of Kandy.

Amidst the many occasions which the distinguished conduct of the army has afforded me of conveying the Sovereign's

Sovereign's approbation, none have exceeded the present event in the sincerity with which I add my congratulations upon your success, and my thanks to yourself and your troops for the exemplary conduct which has led to it.

I have the pleasure to acquaint you, that the Prince Regent has confirmed my recommendation of the officers whose names you have submitted for brevet rank: and his Royal Highness has also been graciously pleased to confer the rank of Lieutenant Colonel in the army upon Major Brownrigg, the bearer of your dispatches.

I am, Sir, yours, &c.
(Signed) FREDERICK,
Commander in Chief.

Lieutenant General
SIR ROBRRT BROWNRIGG, G. C. B.
&c. &c. &c.

By the Lieutenant General's Command,
(Signed) L. D. BUSSCHE,
Act. Dept. Adj. Gen.